cirencester
college
a beacon college

Invitation to Law

INVITATION SERIES

Invitation to Law

A. W. B. Simpson

BASIL BLACKWELL

First published 1988

Basil Blackwell Ltd
108 Cowley Road, Oxford, OX4 1JF, UK

Basil Blackwell Inc.
432 Park Avenue South, Suite 1503
New York, NY 10016, USA

British Library Cataloguing in Publication Data

Simpson, A. W. B.
    Invitation to law. – (Invitation series).
    1. Law
    I. Title
    340   K230

ISBN 0–631–14537–0
ISBN 0–631–14538–9 Pbk

Typeset in 11½ on 12 pt Bembo
by Joshua Associates Limited, Oxford
Printed in Great Britain by
Page Bros. Ltd, Norwich

Contents

Contents

1

The Pervasiveness of Law

A plausible case could easily be made for saying that this book is unnecessary, that law needs no introduction. For, unlike such deep and incomprehensible mysteries as the calculus, semiotics, or catastrophe theory, law is something with which we grew up. Even quite young children, long before they take up shop-lifting, or driving uninsured mopeds, or scrumping apples, are at least familiar with the criminal law, with its court dramas of wickedness and tragedy, its parables of right and wrong, its fearsome denunciations of cruelty and greed. They know only too well what becomes of the likes of Mr Toad and others who violate the more serious rules of social behaviour, once they fall into the hands of the stern and brutal minions of the law. The tales they read, the movies they see, the television they watch, familiarize them with a whole range of conceptions intimately related to the existence of law – pirates and robbers and highwaymen and outlaws in the world of imagination; people who offer sweets and rides in cars, or break into the school over the weekend, at a level closer to reality. They even know, through the story of Robin Hood, that the law can be looked at not as a good thing but as a system of oppression.

Older children and adults know much more than this. In particular their conception of the law is not limited to cops and robbers, for they know that the criminal law forms only a small part of the world of the law and the lawyers. For as we grow older we become familiar with government. And modern government,

1

which obtrudes into a host of everyday activities which have nothing directly to do with crime, operates, at least in large part, through law. In particular it involves the making of new laws and the repealing of old ones, so that elections, which in democracies can change governments, are fought over legislative programmes, and promises of reform of the law embodied in party manifestos. We come to know too that the business of government involves the continuous administration of laws, for example the laws under which unemployed people are entitled to benefits from the state, or the laws which govern immigration into the country from abroad. We learn that many familiar institutions, such as Parliament, the BBC, the Central Electricity Generating Board, the universities, the local councils and a host of commercial companies, are all creatures of the law, with structures and powers and responsibilities ordained by laws.

Though everyday life may rarely if ever have brought most citizens into contact with criminal law, motoring law apart, few can have escaped involvement of some kind with such laws as the tax laws, the laws saying when shops may open, and what age you have to be to purchase liquor, or the laws requiring you to have a passport to travel abroad. Indeed the range of subjects regulated in one way or another by laws is quite extraordinary. There are laws regulating family life (you must not marry your grandmother and if you try it does not work); laws protecting bats from disturbance; laws catering for the welfare of breeding ospreys and for those who wish to have their ears pierced; laws saying that sheep must be dipped whether they or their owners like it or not; laws governing the provision of exits from village halls, and laws requiring food manufacturers to list those awful additives they put in our food, E102 and so forth. Such a list could be extended indefinitely, and there exist comical collections of weird laws, such as the law in Kansas, USA, which forbids you to keep a mule on the first storey of a building, presumably because one once fell out on the mayor. It takes some ingenuity to think of any field of activity which is not in some way or other legally regulated. Sleeping perhaps? Well, no, for you must not sleep whilst driving; and there is a case in the law reports dealing with an American serviceman called Boshears who killed a prostitute, so he said, when he was fast asleep. It caused him some surprise when he woke up, and he managed to convince a jury of this to the amazement of the trial judge who had told the jury (nod nod, wink wink) that if this was so the crime of murder had not been committed, or indeed any other crime, though perhaps a person who made a habit of this might infringe some law or other.

The superabundance of laws reflects today a faith in what can be achieved by them which at times seems to have got quite out of hand; law is the panacea for all social ills. So we have laws to promote racial harmony, and good sex education, and equality between the sexes, and safety at work, and to stamp out insider trading on the Stock Exchange, all admirable ends, and indeed laws to further social justice generally, if only we could all agree on what that requires. And a whole bevy of laws now exists throughout the world to ensure that everyone obtains their human rights, though it must be admitted that these laws do not seem to be conspicuously successful in all parts where they apply, as Amnesty International continuously points out. Never can there have been a time when law was so popular. Hardly a day passes without a call for new laws to stamp out this or that, or further some supposedly desirable end.

We are all, then, aware of the pervasiveness of law. Law, like the air we breathe, is all around us; it is with us from the cradle to the grave, and indeed beyond, grave-robbing being an offence, and wills being enforceable by law. But it is with law as it is with air: most of us know very little about the stuff. Why do we need it, why, for that matter, does there seem at present to be plenty of it about? Is all this talk about acid rain and lead pollution to be taken seriously? Are the sheep near Sellafield wise to take such deep breaths? So it is with the law. People can work all their lives in Imperial Chemical Industries as research chemists, or as receptionists, or whatever, without the slightest knowledge of company law. We can all write cheques without studying the law of negotiable instruments. With minds uncluttered with the legal niceties of the definition of murder or manslaughter, we can keep our hands off our irritating colleagues' throats, and if we do lose our self-control and engage in homicide the reason for this lapse is rarely to be sought in a lack of legal expertise. Though taken for granted, there is something paradoxical about this phenomenon: a society dominated by laws, but one populated by individuals most of whom have only the sketchiest knowledge or understanding of the institution which so pervades their lives. How can this be?

IS LAW PERHAPS UNIMPORTANT?

One possible explanation is that the law is less central to social life and organization than its pervasiveness would suggest. This, at first sight, seems quite a plausible explanation, especially if we concentrate attention upon those branches of the law which are concerned with the prohibition of grossly anti-social behaviour, that is to say with serious crime. Homicide may serve as an example. The law governing homicide, that is killing, is extremely elaborate; it is concerned with murder, with manslaughter, with child destruction, which most people have never heard of, and with other forms of killing which are highly controversial, such as abortion. There exists not only a number of categories of homicide, but in addition a variety of defences to charges of homicide. For example, 'provocation' can reduce a charge of murder to manslaughter, as can a plea of 'diminished responsibility' arising from mental disturbance. Self-defence is a complete answer to a charge, and its precise scope is therefore critically important and carefully worked out; for example, the law says that in the street you must back away from trouble, but in your home, which is your castle, retreat is not required. Hence in Texas murderers, knowing that this rule, exported there, is taken very seriously by jurors in that rugged part of the world, if they are prudent always drag their victims, as soon as life is extinct, into their sitting rooms to lay a basis for their defence. The exact status of some defences is controversial; for example, ought it to be a defence to a charge of murder that the killer was

4

threatened by another that he himself would be killed if he did not kill an innocent victim? Judges have disagreed on the scope of this defence of 'duress'. Some would not allow it in a murder case at all, viewing it as a terrorists' charter. Other judges think it too harsh to call someone a murderer if all they were doing was saving their own life, albeit at someone else's expense. At the moment the official legal view is hostile to this defence, but this may well change. Then there are many rules governing trials for homicide and the sentences which can be passed and the arrangements under which these sentences are served. Large books can be written on the whole subject, and are.

But common sense would suggest that the vast majority of people refrain from assassinating their acquaintances for reasons which owe nothing to the law. They never feel the urge, or feel squeamish, or think it morally wrong, or even believe that they will go to hell when they die if they have taken a human life. In a real sense the law of homicide is wholly irrelevant to most citizens, and conceivably its threats are not very effective on the rare occasions when other social controls over homicidal behaviour are in danger of breaking down; though of course there is no way of being sure how many potential murderers are kept on the straight and narrow each year by the law.

But obviously law is only one of the mechanisms of social control; how we behave is dictated by habits, by traditions, by inherited or instilled inhibitions, by ideals and values, by moral and religious beliefs, by fear of social disapproval, by the desire to be approved of and loved. The heavy hand of the criminal law seems to operate only at the margins of social life, not the centre. But a moment's reflection will suggest that this does not mean that the law of homicide is therefore entirely unimportant. For unfortunately some people do commit murder, and some murderers, such as the Yorkshire Ripper, can have a very serious effect on everyday social life, producing conditions of widespread fear. It is important that society should have some settled way of dealing with such people, something better than the lynch mob and the nearest oak tree, and important too that it should try, through these arrangements, to reduce the incidence of murder, as far as can be achieved. Even a small reduction is a bonus, especially if you are next on the list. The margins of social life are indeed marginal, but still important.

A second and perhaps better reason why law can be of considerable importance, in spite of the fact that most people know little about it, is apparent when the law has been used to alter normal human behaviour, or set up legally regulated artificial institutions, for example the Board of a newly national-ized industry, such as the National Coal Board, formed in 1947. Fairly recently the law required the wearing of seat belts in cars by front seat passengers; for many motorists this was a new form of behaviour introduced into motoring life by the law. Soon after the new regulation came in, and indeed in many cases before it did, motorists developed a habit of buckling up, and what they now conform to is not so much the law as the habit which conforms to it. Law generates habits and practices, and people can conform to such practices with no precise idea of their legal basis. A society which respects the law, and takes it as a guide, will, when some new legal requirement comes into force, soon establish practices which conform to the scheme of legal ordering and regulation, though most people have little idea of the legal basis for them. In much the same way people can drive cars successfully without being able to give the least account of why the choke is needed to start a cold engine, or what the gears do. Universities provide an example of how law operates in this indirect way in the case of institutions. Like commercial companies, universities have elaborately ordained legal struc-tures, embodied in Charters and Ordinances and Regulations. The texts of all this legal material may run to book size, and in my own time those governing the University of Oxford were largely kept in Latin lest anyone should be silly enough to be tempted to read them. But most students and academics neither know nor care about all this mumbo-jumbo. All they need to know about are the practices which apply to them – how to apply for admission, where to pay fees, how to register for a course, where the examinations are held and when. If they do run into difficulty they consult the experts, who are familiar with the rules or know where to look them up. It is indeed the existence of experts which is a large part of the explanation for what seemed at first a puzzling phenomenon: the pervasiveness of law in a society in which there is widespread ignorance of law.

SPECIALIZATION AND EXPERTS

Modern societies involve a high degree of specialization, and this extends to the law just as to other important things, such as sanitary engineering. Without elaborate systems of sewage disposal, which we generally take for granted, modern city life would be ravaged by disease and disfigured by squalor, as was the case in the past. In the bad old days before such systems existed it used to be said that the smell of the River Liffey was one of the sights of Dublin, and the Victorian Thames contrived to surpass it in what was known as The Great Stink of 1858. Today all this is past, and there are fish in the Pool of London again. But most of us have done nothing whatever to bring this about; we leave all but the simplest matters involved in setting up systems of sewage disposal and pollution control to engineers, and call in plumbers when something goes wrong. The participation of most citizens in sewage disposal is largely confined to use, flushing, and the occasional employment of the lavatory brush. Where it all goes, or how on earth it gets there, are mysteries over which we do not trouble our heads. It is much the same with the law as it is with the domestic water closet. When a company is being established company law experts may well be consulted, or their books read, to ensure that we get the system right; once the company is operating recourse to experts will be occasional, perhaps only occurring when matters seem to be going wrong, or some dispute arises. Law, as it functions today, is the job of experts, of lawyers, and indeed without lawyers law as we know it could hardly exist, let alone work, any more than could engineering, or medicine, or computing science, or package holidays on the Costa Brava.

In earlier and simpler forms of society this was not the case.

Knowledge of the right thing to do was not confined, outside the supernatural world, to a special class of person, though older males might in such societies be viewed as better informed than the young, simply because of their greater age and experience of life. But today it is no more possible to have a complex legal system without lawyers than it is possible to have *haute cuisine* without French chefs and Elizabeth David. This does not mean that the law is secret, or that professional lawyers alone possess expert knowledge. Knowledge filters through to many others, to tax consultants, to civil servants, to police officers, to social workers, to doctors, and indeed to professional criminals. In the United States, where very serious attention is given to civil rights, penitentiaries sometimes possess excellent law libraries, so that the incarcerated may know their rights under the constitution. Having little else to do but litigate, some felons become highly expert in criminal and constitutional laws and legal procedure. Similarly with cooking there is, mercifully, a diffusion of expert knowledge. So in many private homes there are cook books by experts to be consulted, and excellent meals to be had, and this is so because knowledge of good cooking has filtered through, as if by some miracle, even into the English home. But that is not where good cooking comes from; it comes from experts. Like chefs, lawyers are expert people who devote their working lives to acquiring and selling special expertise to the public, or, as is the case with judges, to the state. And, again like chefs, they also to some extent create what they sell, and do not simply reproduce what has gone before. In doing so they make the law both more complex and, ideally at least, better.

LAW AND ITS FUNCTIONS

Studying the law through taking courses of formal legal education in a university, or polytechnic, is the most painless way of beginning to acquire the expert knowledge which is the stock in trade of the professional lawyer, and in any event formal legal education is required by the bodies which control the admission of lawyers to practise. But before one sets out to join the club by signing up for such a course it is as well to think a little about what, at least in a general way, the functions of law are or seem to be. In spite of law's pervasiveness not everyone has been encouraged to think much about this, and, so far as school education is concerned, law remains a rather neglected subject.

As is the case with other social institutions the actual effects of law are still not very well understood; we do not know very clearly what differences many laws make to life, for the social sciences, which study such matters, are still not highly developed. If therefore we mean by the functions of law its practical effects, no simple answer is possible. If, on the other hand, by functions we mean the ends which law is supposed to achieve, many thinkers would go along broadly with something like the list of five principal functions which follow. It must be admitted, however, first that with law, as is the case with most social institutions, different people have different ideas as to principal ends for which law exists, or would emphasise some at the expense of others. Secondly, any statement of the functions of law in general has to be expressed, as one might expect, in a very general way. The functions of particular laws may often be set out quite precisely, and may not be controversial at all.

The principal functions of the law are, I should suggest, to be sought in the resolution of conflict, the regulation of human behaviour both to reduce conflict and to further social goals, the distribution of powers, the distribution of property and wealth, and the reconciliation of stability and change. These five general functions can now be examined in a little more detail.

THE RESOLUTION OF CONFLICT

We regularly associate law with the notion of order, as in the catch-phrase 'law and order'. Order is threatened by disputes and conflicts between individuals and groups, particularly if these degenerate into violence. Even a vegetable marrow competition will collapse if the contestants push and shove too much, or, as they are said sometimes to do in Yorkshire, shoot at each other's marrows at night with shot guns. Law provides a formalised mechanism for resolving conflicts, employing that most typical of all legal institutions, the court.

We may dream dreams of human societies in which there are no conflicts, and therefore no need for means of resolving them. Those of the political right tend to romanticise about such utopias in the past, in the good old days of Victorian values for example, whilst those of the political left place Shangri-La in the future, when capitalism has collapsed, a sense of community is restored and everyone contributes to society according to his abilities and receives in return what he needs. The former relate their lost world to respect for law and authority, as essential to social happiness; the latter tend to view law as essentially dispensable, supposing that if the causes for conflict could only be eradicated the need for law would go. Romanticism about conflictless societies has even induced some writers to claim to have discovered actually existing societies of this benign character, as did the late Margaret Mead in her celebrated and entertaining *Growing up in Samoa*, which, when I was a student, was both obligatory reading and received truth. But, as we sadly now know, Miss Mead was taken for a ride by her Samoan informants, an occupational risk with anthropologists, summed up in the West African proverb: 'You do not have to say much to the white man to make him nod his head.' Growing up in Samoa was in fact as rough as it is in England, not the relaxed business depicted by Miss Mead. Real examples of conflictless societies are hard indeed to come by. One claimant, for which I cannot vouch, is the island community of Tristan da Cunha, one of the relics of the British Empire which nobody seems to want. The islanders are said to suppress all social tensions by eating aspirins, achieving harmony at the cost of the highest per capita consumption of salicylic acid in the world. Heaven knows what this does to the linings of their stomachs, but it may save them from courts and lawyers.

If true this story about Tristan has this moral, that courts are only one way of achieving harmony. Indeed many very varied

10

mechanisms for resolving conflicts have been recorded. Some Esquimaux, when matters become tense, perhaps as a result of sexual jealousy and infidelity, sing obscene songs about each other, turn and turn about, until everyone feels better and can go home or return to the seal hunt. For a conflict is resolved if it ceases to have a disruptive effect, however this is brought about. Similar practices, which transform the underlying dispute into a less damaging traditional and acceptable form, survive today; think of formalised abuse in family rows, or listen to the radio when transmitting a lively House of Commons debate, or Prime Minister's question time. It sounds like a zoo, but may be valuable for all that, for we are assured that Members of the House repair afterwards to the bars to drink together in a friendly manner.

More elaborate mechanisms for getting conflicts to go away may include the use of an agreed umpire, a mediator, or an arbitrator. The *umpire* simply regulates the way the obscene singing goes on, for example making sure that turns are taken. A *mediator* actively intervenes to seek a compromise or some agreed solution. An *arbitrator* is someone who, with the consent of the parties, actually decides the dispute. With arbitration we are close to *adjudication* and the idea of a court. Courts, which involve adjudication, differ from these other mechanisms in four important ways.

First, they have *authority* to intervene and decide what is to be done even without the joint consent of the parties. So courts can only exist in societies which recognize hierarchies of power; they cannot exist in societies which are wholly egalitarian, where nobody, outside the family, has power over anyone else. Second, they *decide* who is right and who is wrong, and what is to be done. They do not simply *suggest*, or *recommend*, or *persuade*. In so far as their authority is voluntarily accepted as legitimate, this presents no problems, but if someone refuses to knuckle under the whole system of adjudication is under threat. Hence courts only exist in societies where there are very powerful motives for submission to them, and in the modern world this means that their authority is backed by force. There must be both a general acceptance of the idea that resort to a court is the proper way of settling disputes which cannot be settled in some other way, and coercion of those who reject the authority of the system. Third, courts are thought of as standing outside the conflict, and as deciding or adjudicating upon the dispute objectively, by reference to some standard which existed before the decision and will continue to exist after it. If the court says the plaintiff is in the right, this is because he really is, in a timeless sense, in the right, not because the judge happens to be friends with him, or thinks that from his point of view this is the best solution. This objectivity is something which helps to secure submission to the decision; it is to be submitted to because it is right. Early courts solved the problem of objectivity by channelling the decision up to an omnisicient God, who, being in possession of all the facts, knows the guilt or innocence of a person accused of crime, for example, and revealed the truth through such mechanisms as the ordeal. The accused person might have to carry a hot object, blessed by the priest, a certain number of paces; if his hand healed then this showed that God exonerated him. In civil cases the same basic technique employed the formal battle, in which God would intervene to see that right prevailed. In more modern times objectivity is sought in the idea that cases must be settled rationally, that there must be good reasons for deciding the dispute one way rather than another, reasons which will apply to all similar cases in the future. Fourth, courts as we now know them are run by professional experts, though these may be associated in some way with non-experts, as is the case with the jury.

If courts are to be recognizable institutions, distinguishable from birthday parties, or debating clubs, they have to follow settled procedures; it is these procedures which mark a court off from a lynch mob. Since it is of the essence of these court procedures that they differ from other social reactions to trouble the law becomes viewed as a distinct and separate segment of social life. Today legal procedures regulating courts, which are extremely complicated, are still of paramount importance in the practice of the law; in earlier times the law which the experts administered consisted of virtually nothing else. For these early courts accepted whatever social rules of behaviour, standards of right and wrong, and ideas of who is entitled to what, existed in the society in which they operated. So much was taken as given. Courts simply tried to pick up the pieces when trouble broke out, by establishing and following settled *procedures* which helped to bring a dispute to the point of resolution in a tidy way.

When law is at this stage of development it is merely remedial. The law does not lay down standards of proper social behaviour; it merely provides ways of going about things when, through neglect of proper standards, things go wrong. This aspect of law survives, and even today we can look at much of our law as remedial only. Take again the example of homicide. It is surely a distortion to think that it is the law which tells us not to murder; we know that already. Instead the law sets out in detail what is to be done about it if somebody does murder. Again the law does not tell us to drive on the left of the road; the rule is traditional and conventional, and part of being British. The law does however have a lot to say about what is to be done if we drive on the right and have an accident. We may say that law of this remedial character, which concentrates upon procedure only, is engaged in merely *reinforcing* standards of behaviour which exist quite independently of it, being based upon custom or convention or ethics or religious belief. It does so by setting out a sequence of appropriate reactions to mis-conduct and wrongdoing. Those who murder are to be arrested, brought before a magistrates' court, committed for trial at the Crown Court, tried by a jury in accordance with the rules of criminal evidence, if convicted sentenced to imprisonment for life, given a chance to appeal, et cetera.

From merely reinforcing existing standards, it is a short step to refining them. Instead of the courts simply saying what is to happen to murderers, the experts who deal with murderers may begin to develop their own ideas as to what is to count as murder. They begin to sharpen up customary or conventional or ethical conceptions and standards; they begin to develop their own definitions of murder. In the common law system this began

13

when jury trial began to supersede divine and therefore infallible modes of trial, for jurymen could obviously make mistakes. The experts become nervous about leaving to the laymen the whole business of adjudication, for example not only the decision as to what the accused had done, but also whether it ought to count as murder. So they began to take over the job of adjudication, at least in part. Thus what is to count as murder becomes a matter for the experts to settle, what we call a question of law.

With this development the law takes on a new character, becoming concerned with the substance of social ordering, not merely with the processes of dispute resolution. Under the guise of merely making more precise conceptions which exist in popular consciousness quite independently of the law, such as theft or robbery, the lawyers, and the law, are now specifying standards of right and wrong behaviour, for it is what the lawyers say is theft or robbery which is, so far as courts are concerned, what matters. This leads to the development of what are called legal concepts, concepts which differ from lay concepts in sharpness and scope.

Murder is a typical example of such a legal concept. The everyday idea of a murderer is vague and centres around the notion of a deliberate, premeditating, killer. Such is the murderer of detective stories, or the murderer who, in our imagination, lurks in the woods at night. The legal concept of murder is much wider. Thus it includes a person who keeps watch whilst someone else does the killing. It even includes people who do not mean to kill anyone at all, but merely to injure other people seriously. Nor does the law require any premeditation in the sense of planning. Many killings which count as murders in the law arise out of sudden quarrels and loss of temper, often in domestic situations, without any prior planning at all. There is a sense in which some such killings are really accidental. Although the matter is currently controversial, the law has in the past even counted as murder killings which were accidental in an even stronger sense, in that the accused had no intention even to injure. This used to be the law when death accidentally occurred in the course of a robbery, or a rape, or an illegal abortion; it was automatically murder. Even very recently the law was equally harsh on those who took serious risks in illegitimate enterprises; they could be convicted of murder even though they never meant to hurt anyone at all. So lawyers' murder, and layman's murder, were not the same thing at all, though they overlapped.

The process which creates legal concepts, and distinct lawyers' ideas of right and wrong, and of who is entitled to what, leads to a separation between legal standards and other standards; we can lump together these other standards and call them popular moral standards. Matters of right and wrong, of who is entitled to what, deal with the substance of social order, and legal standards of this character are called standards of *substantive* law, as opposed to standards of procedure only. The experts who run the courts, the lawyers, when they justify what they do, do so by reference to a body of ideas which they have themselves developed and elaborated, and which comes to be seen as distinct from popular moral standards. It is this distinct body of ideas which is what lawyers mean by the law. The significance and importance of these ideas depends, in the first instance, not upon their being accepted by society at large, but upon their being accepted by the experts.

We often think of law as a body of rules, rather like school rules, telling us all, as citizens, how to behave, and what will happen if we do not. But this is not the way lawyers primarily think of their law. For lawyers the function of law is to tell *them* how to behave in settling what people's rights and duties and obligations and liabilities are. The elaborate body of general principles, the more detailed rules and the exceptions to them, the definitions of terms and significant distinctions, the practices and conceptions which to lawyers constitute the law, are there to provide lawyers with ways of analysing problems, and ways of rationally justifying decisions as to what is to be done by courts about them. Law is for lawyers.

Courts, where these special ideas develop, are like other social institutions in being much influenced by tradition, by what has been done in the past, by the way matters have, as it is said, always been done. So one way of claiming objectivity in the law has always been to say that the decisions taken are in line with how things have always been. The alternative has been to claim, more simply, that the decision in question is rational in itself. The practice of justification in a world which combines traditional procedures (how we go about things) and traditional or supposedly intrinsically rational rules of decision (how disputes should be analysed and correctly resolved) creates the artificial world of legal categories, into which disputes and quarrels may be translated and, so translated, authoritatively determined.

THE DIRECT REGULATION OF BEHAVIOUR BY LAW

Once the lawyers get into the game of refining existing ideas of right and wrong, and entitlement, it is a further short step, though one of critical importance, to using the coercive power of courts, and the respect which may exist for them as objective deciders, to initiate deliberate change in the standards of behaviour, or rules of entitlement, existing in society. This may involve either changing old rules, or introducing quite new ones. An example of the latter would be a law introducing an income tax. This step gives rise to legislation, deliberate law making, and to legislatures, bodies with admitted power to make laws, whose force as law is conceived of as depending not on the justifications which are offered for it, but upon the authority of the source from which it comes, often called the will of the legislature. Law ceases to be something which just exists, it becomes something which can be made. Legislatures everywhere develop out of courts, and even today the British Parliament, our principal legislature, is properly called The High Court of Parliament. This name, which has persisted, reflects the original chaaracter of the institution as an adjudicative body. The evolution of law making is assisted by the very blurred and indistinct line which exists between the work of a court in saying what the law, as something existing objectively, is, and, by authoritatively determining what it is, actually creating law. With avowed law making comes the institutional division between courts, which continue to claim that they merely say what the law, objectively, is, and law-making bodies which do not make this claim.

Most human societies, at most stages of their history, have had little explicit and avowed law making. What law making there has been may have been viewed as merely correcting defects in the working of the law, rather than changing it. But today legal machinery is employed on a massive scale to govern society by the deliberate making of new laws, which are then enforced by officials working, ultimately, through the courts. So courts have come to be the servants of legislation, and law, once viewed as a means for resolving trouble in a society whose broad structures were given and part of the natural order of things, comes to be viewed as a mechanism for changing and improving the world.

Modern government of course employs other weapons as well as law – exhortation, the manipulation of public opinion by press releases, leaked information, advertisements such as those used in the campaign to restrict the spread of Aids, and what the Cabinet Secretary has called the 'economical use of the truth', not to mention occasional bribery and bullying. But its principal avowed mechanism is the law. So the rise in the scope of government has gone hand in hand with a massive rise in law making. With this too comes a new conception of law as an instrument for change, for reform, for improvement, for producing a different sort of society. Objects currently pursued through the mechanism of the law include the reduction in unemployment, the improvement of health, the happiness of animals, the encouragement of scientific research, the reduction in the frequency of erotic thoughts (called by lawyers libidinous thoughts), the preservation of fish stocks, and in general what is called the regulation of the economy. Law has come a long way from its modest beginnings as a means of keeping the peace.

LAW AND THE DISTRIBUTION OF POWER

Courts, as we have seen, entail an unequal distribution of power in society. The authority of a court consists in its superiority over the litigants. If you go to court you can see this inequality dramatized and symbolised by wigs and gowns, and peculiar architectural levels, and Royal Arms, and an amazing amount of deferential behaviour, bowing and scraping and standing up and sitting down. It may be that all this symbolism helps to generate, through what is called the majesty of the law, submission to the system.

Early societies, such as that in which the common law originated, as well as providing for the administration of justice through courts also organized war and taxation, and these divisions of government again involved hierarchies of power, with generals to command armies, and tax collectors to bring in the money. Today, with the extension of government, a host of officials possess special powers denied to the rest of us. Think of policemen and policewomen, chief constables, building inspectors, ministers of the Crown, customs officers. Officials only are officials because they possess special powers conferred by law. Legal rules specify, with a greater or less degree of precision, who they are and what these powers are. In this way the law prescribes the structures of authority through which government, as we know it, is carried on.

Here as elsewhere in modern society there is much specialization of function. Instead of everyone in government being a jack of all trades there are ambassadors and health officers and coroners, all with their own role and set of powers, and, often, duties too. This makes possible another feature of the system. The inequalities of power only apply to part of the official's life, the official part. The British Ambassador in Paris is my superior when it comes to issuing me with a replacement passport, but if he tries punching me on the nose when we meet on holiday in Cornwall he will find that for that purpose we remain equals. This is what is meant by the rather misleading expression 'equality before the law'. The fact of the matter is that people are not equal before the law, and if they were we would be living in a state of anarchy, and not under government by law at all. What is meant is first that we think of unequal powers as exceptional departures from a natural state of equality, and, second, that there is no class of persons who are in every aspect of their lives, or even in most, specially privileged, so as to be generally above the law. Even to this there are curious exceptions. The Queen herself is, as things stand, above the law; that is why she pays no taxes. And foreign diplomats, under what is called diplomatic immunity, are too. One of the problems this causes is that diplomats from some countries pay little attention to parking regulations. But being immune from the law does not make them immune from the Denver Boot, which is enthusiastically affixed to their vehicles by traffic wardens so as to bring home to them that law and reality are two different worlds.

Not all powers conferred by law are governmental. Parents have power over their children, property owners over their property, and by agreement and collaboration, which lawyers call *contract*, private citizens can establish little commonwealths – golfing associations for recreation, political pressure groups like the Campaign for Nuclear Disarmament, philanthropic societies dedicated to the welfare of children such as the National Society for the Prevention of Cruelty to Children, frivolous organizations like the Permissive Society – each with its power structure of presidents and chairpersons and treasurers and committees. The law reinforces these relationships of power. Thus parental power is protected by the punishment of kidnappers, property owners by the restraint of trespassers, club structures by the incarceration of treasurers who run off with the funds. The law also sets limits to its involvement; hang gliding is one thing, murder incorporated quite another. Relationships of power are also involved in employment contracts, and here in modern times there has been much legislation modifying the power relationships which would exist if purely market forces were allowed to operate.

THE DISTRIBUTION OF WEALTH AND ENTITLEMENTS

Closely associated with the distribution of power is the distribution of wealth, that is to say allocating things which people want and value, such as houses and cars and pet dogs and jobs and copyright in video recordings and holidays in the sun. One principal body of law engaged in this business is the law of property. This provides rules which can be applied to determine what is mine and what is thine, rules determining what sorts of things can be mine or thine (no slaves are allowed today though they once were), rules saying how things become mine or thine (if you hit a pheasant on a motorway can you pick it up and cook it?), and rules as to how things, once mine, become thine (for example by being left to you in a will). The law does not simply allocate forms of wealth, such as paintings by Pablo Picasso, which could exist and be physically possessed and defended and used even without law. It also seems to make certain forms of wealth possible which could hardly exist without law. This is particularly striking in the case of what is called intangible property, such as copyright in a movie. Copyright only has a value, so that it can be sold, because the law protects it. It is hard to see how it could be defended without the organized protection of the law. A strong and vigilant person could keep a tight grip upon something tangible and keep others off it, but it is hard to see how anyone could protect his copyright by physical force; he would need to be everywhere at once. In modern society much wealth consists in intangible property, as the affluence of pop stars shows; it is by selling copyright that they acquire Rolls-Royces.

The rules of property law are extremely complicated and need to be, because of the complexity of life, as may be illustrated by the following problem upon which I was once consulted.

A shooting club had by contract acquired the right to shoot pheasants on some farmland adjacent to the home of a school-teacher, who strongly objected to blood sports. One of the shooters fired at a wild flying pheasant which was at that moment above the farmland but, at the moment of firing, altered course to head towards the schoolteacher's property; the hapless bird was hit and fell into the schoolteacher's garden, but the precise moment of its decease was not known; it may have died in flight or perhaps on striking the ground, or even languished for some moments thereafter. The shooter demanded the right to collect 'his bird' which had, through its own perversity, landed in the garden but had, he claimed, been killed on the farmland. The schoolmaster refused permission, saying the bird was either his, or belonged to nature, and expressed himself in no uncertain terms on the subject of blood sports. The shooter ignored him, pushed him away, entered the property and removed the bird, offering with mock humility to pay for any damage he might have caused. The schoolmaster sued him for trespass, and reported him to the police for theft, poaching and assault. Tempers ran high on both sides. The law has to have some sort of answer to such a problem, and one that is consistent with other answers it gives: devising one is inherently tricky and complex.

Yet in spite of the complexity both of the issues and the law the practices associated with property ownership are so well understood and established, and the allocations of property so generally respected, that the need to consult experts occurs remarkably rarely. Lawyers only feature prominently in the transfer of landed property, the making of wills and in the more important transactions involving companies. As for the courts they are involved in property disputes very rarely indeed. Given the law, most disputes are settled by negotiation, in the knowledge that a solution by litigation is always a possible last resort.

The law of property is not the only branch of the law which deals with the allocation of wealth. The law of contract regulates and polices transactions in which it is agreed that property shall be exchanged, as in a sale. Indeed many forms of wealth consist in the benefit of a contract. The whole institution of credit – and remember that it is credit that is used to pay for much of what we acquire, from refrigerators to houses – depends upon contractual obligations. No doubt in a world peopled only by saints whose word was their bond we could have credit without law, but in the real world which contains villains too, the legal coercion of the disreputable underlies the faith we put in the system.

Property rights and contractual rights are obviously forms of wealth; so too are rights under trusts. So the branches of the law which deal with these rights are plainly concerned in the business of wealth allocation, and indirectly the allocation of power, for the ownership of property brings power with it. It is not quite so obvious that the law, whenever it restricts our freedom to do as we wish, is in a sense determining the distribution of wealth. For example, if the law forbids me to sell heroin, it prevents me from selling my services as a drug pedlar, at which I may be very good, and condemns me to the more modestly remunerated life of a university teacher. Again if you live in an old house which has been officially listed as a Grade I historic building, the law severely restricts what alterations you may carry out; if you want to add a new floor you may be prevented from doing so. In this the law is taking away from you something you value, and giving the public, or your neighbours, something which they may value, the pleasure of looking at a beautiful building, or preserving for future generations the chance of living in one. They have not paid for this. Of course the law may actually enhance the value of the property; either way it has economic effects. Again if a law is passed allowing an airline to fly low over my home and abolishing my previous right to sue the airline for nuisance, the value of my house drops and the airline gains: its costs of operation fall. So there has been a transfer of wealth, a change in previously existing entitlements. Whether this is just or desirable depends upon how you view the distribution of wealth before the transfer was made, and what force you give to the reasons for the transfer. Problems of this sort are often talked about in terms of a conflict between individual interest and the public interest, but really the conflict is simply between individuals. There is no such animal as 'the public'.

THE RECONCILIATION OF STABILITY AND CHANGE

One of the most paradoxical features of law is that it operates both as a means of preserving the status quo and as a means of introducing deliberate change in our social arrangements.

Like so many features of the world we live in, such as our roads, our homes, our religious beliefs and our language, law is essentially a tradition, that is to say something which has come down to us from the past. Some features of the law derive from the very distant past indeed. In English law, for example, the terms which are in use for talking about property rights in land are medieval; most of them would be perfectly intelligible to a fifteenth-century lawyer. So lawyers when they are being technical do not talk of *landowners*, but of *tenants in fee simple absolute in possession*, of *fees tail* and even more mysterious entities such as *possibilities of reverter*. There is even a poem about some of them:

> Fee simple, and the shifting fees,
> And all the fees in tail,
> Are nothing when compared to thee,
> Thou best of fees, female.

Again much of the present structure and language of contract law is even older than that, and was derived by a roundabout route from the writings of lawyers in the Roman Empire; of course there are other branches of the law, for example welfare law, which have a very much shorter intellectual history. The traditional character of the law does not mean that the law is necessarily inconveniently archaic, any more than the English language suffers from its inheritance from the past, though it may happen in the law that old rules survive when the point of them has long gone. This comes about when lawyers become victims and not masters of their tradition. One of the skills of a great judge is an ability to make the new wine come out of the old bottles, ideally without people being too aware of what is going on.

Although today there is much talk of governments changing the law, this does not affect the traditional character of law. For the vast bulk of the law soldiers on under successive governments, little altered; there is neither the time, the inclination, nor the need to change it. Furthermore there is usually some group which does well out of the law as it is, and seeks to maintain its advantageous position. Law then is one of the mechanisms which contribute to the rule of the past over the present. So it is that I own my house now, today, because I bought it under a mortgage *in the past*, and the relevant law has remained the same. It would be most inconvenient if this were not the case. This stabilising influence of the law to some degree benefits everyone; imagine if the rule of the road kept changing each week. But it also has its dark side. For example, in a society in which wealth is unevenly distributed, and this is true of all modern societies, whatever the system of government under which they operate, the law's protection of property rights obviously in a sense favours the haves over the have nots. Even the have nots will own some property, and benefit from its protection, and the less property you own the more critically important its protection becomes. Elaborate theories exist which claim that in the long term everyone benefits from stable property rights – for example, allowing people to keep what they have earned may provide incentives to individuals to work hard and create more wealth, from which the whole society benefits in the end. Not everyone finds these theories very convincing; one problem is that the protection of property rights always has to start from some initial distribution, and its effects are conditioned by whatever this was. As a bitter Texan farmer is said to have remarked recently, 'You can make a small fortune in farming, so long as you start with a large one.'

In so far as law protects the status quo its operators, the lawyers, represent a conservative force in society. But the law does and has to change, and in the process rights and entitlements and power are reallocated in society. Avowed change by legislation, and the more gradual and largely unavowed change by the development of the law by the courts, are both mechanisms for peaceable and regular change in response either to movements in opinion or political activity. Changing the law through mechanisms provided by the law is an alternative to the *coup d'état*, or to thoroughgoing revolution, and also an alternative to situations in which, although there is no revolution, social harmony breaks down. So not only courts but law itself is a mechanism for the resolution of conflicts within society. Examples of very important legal changes in Britain include the passing of the 1832 Reform Act, which, arguably, headed off the threat of violent revolution, or the introduction of the modern Welfare State by the Labour government of 1945. Change of a dramatic nature by court decision is better illustrated by American history, for in America the system of government both inhibits legislative change and gives a greater role to the courts. A striking example is the decision of the US Supreme Court in the case of *Brown* v. *The Board of Education* in l954, which ended racially segregated public education, and, along with other factors, appears to have dramatically improved the lot of black Americans in the southern states, though its effect upon the educational system was not entirely as expected. If societies are to prosper, stability and change have to be reconciled, and one function of the law is to effect this reconciliation by channelling change through peaceable procedures.

LAW, VIOLENCE AND COERCION

If these, or something like them, are the principal functions of law a word needs to be said about its methods. As we have seen and can see every day of the week, citizens in the main co-operate with the law, albeit sometimes after a little prompting, such as the final demand from the Electricity Board. Even those who get into trouble with the law almost all co-operate at some point or other; they may come quietly when arrested, or confess all, they go peacefully to prison or even, in the awful days of capital punishment, to the scaffold. Albert Pierrepoint, our last hangman, records that he only recalled one hanging at which the victim, a German spy, resisted violently. Many historical examples exist of condemned individuals who, in their last speech, extolled the justice of their sentence, and an early seventeenth-century example exists of an individual who, when his hand was cut off, waved the bloody stump, fresh from the boiling tar, in the air crying, 'God Save the Queen.' No doubt one reason for this is that people do accept the idea that they ought, morally, to obey the law and conform to its demands, even against their own immediate self-interest. There are no doubt other reasons. A legal system is in deep trouble if this voluntary acceptance begins to fail. One way the law fosters it is by presenting itself and its authority as legitimate, its decisions as fair and just, its rules and doctrines as wise, its judges as honourable, unbiased and humane, if stern. Hence it is that a great deal of legal activity involves justification. The law also must present itself as embodying irresistible power, so that resistance to it is pointless. Hence the general rule of the police – never get into a fight unless you are sure to win it. There is even a grim legal maxim followed in the old court of Chancery expressing this idea: 'Equity does nothing in vain.'

But there will always be individuals who are not prepared to conform, whether it is because they are bad, or bloody minded, or selfish, or perhaps because they genuinely believe that the system lacks moral authority, or that some particular law or legal decision does. All legal systems whatsoever make provision for this problem by the use of coercive force or the threat of it. Only occasionally do we see this in operation, for example during the miners' strike when films of police charges filled the television screens. But the possibility is always there.

Coercive force is not the same thing as punishment, though some punishments have involved force, for example flogging. Taking this disagreeable example, the *punishment* was the flogging; the *coercive force* is the violence used to compel the wretched individual to be flogged. The abolition of violent punishments, such as flogging, branding, amputation and hanging, has not in any way abolished the use of coercive force to secure submission to the law. Try persistently playing a trombone in the Court of Appeal (Criminal Division) and see what happens to you after the initial courteous request to desist has failed.

Of course it is not the law, some bloodless abstraction, which will drag you off; officials exist whose job it is to do this. What the law does is to establish rules which differentiate between legitimate violence (warders dragging a convicted bank robber to the Black Maria) and illegitimate violence (the robber fighting back). It does this by banning all violence and then making exceptions, here an exception in favour of the warders, who cannot be sued or prosecuted for what they do. This is sometimes put by saying that the law, or the state, *monopolises* the use of violence. But this is a mistake; much violence occurs in boxing or rugby football quite lawfully. What it monopolises is the decision as to when violence is allowed, and its decision is self-interested. The law is allowed to use violence but others, as a general rule, are not, and you are never allowed to use violence deliberately against the law.

Many students find the idea that the law is itself backed by force or threats of force, applied most obviously by the police, a disagreeable idea; they feel that law ought to be in its very nature at odds with violence, and this feeling may explain the tendency to play down this embarrassing fact about the law. The problems associated with the policing of inner city areas, and the disturbances which have occurred in some of them, have recently highlighted both the law's ultimate dependence upon coercion and the unhappy results which follow when policing by consent appears to have broken down, and the use of coercive force becomes more regular. But isolated uses of coercive force, which occur all over the country every day of the week, do not in the same way obtrude upon our attention.

2

Legal Ideals and Sordid Realities

Human beings live in part by ideals, and lawyers are no exception to this. Of course it does not follow that lawyers necessarily live up to these ideals; unfortunately they do not. There are crooked lawyers, just as there are crooked accountants, cowardly soldiers and promiscuous priests. As for doctors I have myself been operated upon by a sadistic doctor without the benefit of an anaesthetic whilst on holiday in Italy. Instead of nitrous oxide or ether he employed two large nuns who sat upon me murmuring *coraggio* from time to time whilst he, with pleasurable slowness, hacked away with a scalpel which seemed to be near the end of its useful life. So we must not expect too much of lawyers, any more than we do of other professionals; indeed a case might be made for saying that each profession is associated with its own peculiar forms of depravity. Consider politicians. Furthermore, human beings have such powers of self-deception that they may convince themselves they are behaving in accordance with their avowed ideals, although they are not. But all this does not mean that the ideals associated with the practice of the law are unimportant; indeed it is quite impossible to understand law as a social institution without knowing something about them. This is true even for those who adopt a wholly cynical attitude, and who believe, as some legal sceptics do, that the legal profession's claim to pursue ideals through the law is simply a device which blinds both lawyers and their victims to the grim reality of the matter: that the law, far from being A Good Thing, is A

Thoroughly Bad Thing. We shall return to these sceptics at the end of this chapter.

What then are these ideals? Ideals are something more fundamental than mere codes of professional ethics. Such codes state standards which all lawyers are expected to follow; ideals are much less attainable than that. Now lawyers possess no equivalent of the Hippocratic Oath. There is no official statement to consult, and we must expect any statement of the ideals which inspire human behaviour to be rather imprecise and also abstract. By way of example, consider Walter Savage Landor's well-known epitaph, in which he tried to set out, in a rather pompous way, the ideals which had, in his own view, shaped his life:

> I strove with none, for none deserved my strife.
> Nature I loved, and next to nature, art,
> I warmed my hands before the fire of life,
> It sinks, and I am ready to depart.

Neither 'nature' nor 'art' is a very precise concept, but it does not follow that Landor's claim was specious. The same is true of the lawyer's principal ideals: *justice*, and *the rule of law*. Some would add a third principal ideal, *law and order*, though, as we shall see, it is not clear that this should have the same elevated status.

Both these first two ideals derive from the ancient world. The Greeks, who were good at philosophy, said most of what can be said about justice, though some of what they said is not easy to follow today because their basic idea was that justice was a personal quality possessed by just men, whereas we tend to think of it primarily as a quality of social arrangements. They also said a certain amount about the rule of law and respect for law, and the story of the trial and submission of Socrates has these ideas as its theme. But it was the Romans, here as elsewhere practically minded, who developed and actually operated the notion of a society under the rule of law, which notion later Europeans have both acted out and elaborated to form what is called liberal political theory.

JUSTICE AND LAW

Justice, of all the virtues, is the virtue peculiarly associated with the law. Like truth or beauty it is something we are all in favour of, but it is by no means easy to say what it is. One possible way of teasing out the notions involved is to distinguish a number of different senses in which we commonly use the idea.

One sense in which we talk about justice seems to make justice and law mean much the same thing, for example when we call a court of law a court of justice, or talk about the administration of justice, when we could as well have talked about the administration of law. In this same sense many countries have Ministers of Justice. If justice is some sort of moral virtue this sounds not a little odd or even comical, as if we had a Ministry of Truth, or a Department of Courage. One would expect them to deal in lies and cowardice. But the reason why we use the idea of justice in this way, as synonymous with law, is that the central concern of justice is that of ensuring that people receive what they are entitled to, and what they deserve, and these seem to be central concerns of that most typical of all legal institutions, the court. What else are courts for? So this is why we use the terms justice and law as synonymous; the practice reflects the idea that the connection between law and justice is one that exists in the very nature of things, because of the purposes inherent in the very institution of law itself.

A second sense is often given the title 'justice according to law'. According to this a person obtains justice if he gets whatever it is he is really entitled to under the law, or suffers whatever penalty the law provides for him. So a murderer obtains justice if he is convicted, sentenced and punished according to law; a creditor who is owed £100 obtains justice if he gets his hundred pounds. And frequently we say that someone was denied justice, for example if a court sentenced him without attending to his plea in mitigation, of if he is too poor to bring a case in court. Conforming to this notion of justice according to law, the decision of a court may obviously involve injustice; an

30

innocent person may be convicted instead of the real murderer, or the creditor may have in reality already been paid the money. In such circumstances reality and the legal decision are not in tune, or we could say that the purpose of the law, which is to convict the guilty and ensure the payment of real debts, has not been achieved. So justice according to law is a critical notion, in the sense that it can be used to evaluate a legal decision by comparing what actually has happened with what, ideally, ought to have happened.

Sometimes it is said that justice according to law is a merely procedural conception: so long as the court has observed the rules then the decision is just, even if the man is innocent, or the debt not due. But this, though comforting to judges who have, in good faith, sentenced an innocent person to punishment, is a mistake, for the ideal of justice according to law goes to the substance of the matter, not just to forms and procedures. The matter is confused by the use of the unfortunate expression 'formal justice' to describe justice according to law, an expression that suggests that so long as the legal forms have been gone through we have justice according to law, which is not correct. The pursuit of justice according to law requires lawyers, and especially judges, to administer the law conscientiously, and with careful regard for its purpose. Mere conformity with legal forms will not do. The idea, it will be noticed, presupposes that there is both some way of telling what the law is, and of settling what its aims are. If these things are possible then a judge can simply dedicate himself to the conscientious application of the law. But if there are situations in which the law is uncertain, or its purposes obscure, a judge has something more to do than this. He has to pursue justice in a different sense.

This different third sense in which we use the idea of justice involves a critical attitude to the law, which is external to it in a more radical sense, for it starts from the assumption that the laws themselves may be just or unjust. So a person may obtain justice according to law, but the legal decision may nevertheless be an unjust one, if the law itself is unjust, or if it leaves the judge with a discretion which he has exercised unjustly. This more radically critical conception of justice, sometimes called substantial justice, is also often called fairness. It rests upon three basic ideas. The first is that of equality, the second is that of desert and the third is that of moral or natural entitlement. All are problematical ideas, but ones which we nevertheless regularly use in discussion and argument about the law and about social arrangements, probably every day of the week.

Justice as *equality* (sometimes called equity) is the idea that it is proper that like cases should be treated alike, or to put it another way that people should be treated equally unless there is some significant and relevant difference between their cases. Appeal to this idea is endlessly made in everyday life, as when children complain that 'Susan was allowed to stay up late when she was ten and I'm ten now', or when adults complain that they were fined £15 for speeding but their friend was only fined £12 for 'exactly the same thing'. In the world of the law a massive part of legal argument involves disputes as to whether or not two cases are alike, or in some relevant way different. There is a simple explanation for this intimate connection between justice as equality, and law. Suppose, for example, that we agree that all human beings are equal in one respect, which is that they have a moral right to an adequate diet. We can express this in the form of a rule: all human beings ought to have an adequate diet. Or suppose we agree that all people in Britain who are over the age of sixty, whose income falls below £40 per week are alike in so far as their claim to state aid for heating is concerned. We can again obviously express this in the form of a rule: all people who are alike in being over sixty and having an income below £40 per week shall receive aid for heating bills. The rule can then specify how much aid. Now rules are what the law seems to be all about; it operates with rules. So justice as equality seems to require rules setting out how categories of people ('murderers', 'all human beings', 'children') should be treated ('locked up for life', 'given enough to eat', 'given a proper education'), and rules of this sort seem to be the business of the law. Indeed according to one way of looking at the matter, law just consists in rules of this kind of a very elaborate nature, and nothing else.

One serious catch with justice as equality is that people may not agree on how to decide what differences between people are relevant and justify different treatment. Ought all murderers to be treated the same? Or are some (poisoners perhaps, or murderers of small children) worse than others? Ought all citizens to pay local taxes, or only householders? Much political controversy is about issues of this kind. A topical example is race. History is of course full of examples of regimes which have treated racial differences between people as so critical that members of certain races were not really treated as people at all. The Nazi regime treated Jews in this way, with appalling consequences; the South African regime treats black people as so different as not to be capable of sharing political power with whites, a view which the black people and many white people too find quite unacceptable. I guess that the majority of those who read this book would agree, and find what is called racialism very offensive. On the other hand they would probably also agree that some differences between people ought to justify different treatment. For example, they might agree that people who are seriously mentally disturbed, or suffering from serious heart conditions, ought not to be allowed to fly aeroplanes. Is there some way of settling in an objective way which differences should matter, and which not? Is there, in theory at least, a definitive list of relevant differences for particular purposes? Some people have felt that if any sense is to be made of the notion of justice as equality there needs to be. They would like it to be possible to demonstrate in some way that racialism is quite definitely wrong. Others are inclined to think that views on this matter are simply subjective and relative, but to concede this seems to deprive criticism of racialism of much of its moral force.

In practice, although no two cases are ever entirely alike, there will often be widespread agreement within a society that some differences are, for some purposes, quite irrelevant. For example, take age, as relevant to criminal liability. Most people would agree that very young children who kill other people ought not to be treated as criminals. Age is a relevant factor, though there may be trouble about settling the precise age. But everyone would surely agree that it would be silly to have one law of murder for forty-one-year-olds and a different one for forty-two-year-olds, there being no rational principle to which one could appeal to justify treating this difference in age as relevant to the matter in hand, though it might make sense for some other purposes, such as regular checking of blood pressure. Again, sometimes arguments as to which differences are relevant come down to factual disagreements. Take our South African example. The supporters of apartheid claim that black people are, as a matter of fact, both different and inferior, whilst accepting the proposition that if this were not so then equal treatment would be appropriate. Such a claim can perhaps be shown so conclusively to be false that even the apartheid supporters change their view, and thus the controversy may be laid to rest. In the South African context this seems a lot to hope for, since people's factual beliefs are so strongly coloured by their social attitudes, but strange beliefs once widely held have been laid to rest in this way. For example, the celebrated father of penology, Cesare Lombroso, thought that criminals were atavistic throwbacks to primitive man, and could be spotted by such physical peculiarities as the shape of their ear lobes, and, in men, the development of their breasts. Havelock Ellis popularized this idea in Britain in a book, *The Criminal*, which now seems hilarious, for today such ideas are thought to be rubbish. A British government report produced devastating evidence against Lombroso's ideas; it checked up on criminals' physical make-up and this just did not fit the theory. So today nobody would want to treat people differently in the criminal law because they had funny ear lobes. Conceivably some racial beliefs will go the same way.

So justice as equality throws up all sorts of intellectual problems, some of an intractable nature, but in Western thought belief in justice as equality does do something very basically important: it puts on the defensive anyone who denies the basic underlying moral notion of human equality. It places the burden of proof on those who seek to support unequal treatment.

Societies which have never accepted this assumption of human equality as even a hypothesis are uneasy with the idea.

The second idea underlying conceptions of substantial justice is that of *desert*. We think, for example, that people who do good things, like rescuing children who have fallen into ponds, or organizing charitable appeals for people suffering from starvation, deserve something good in return, such as thanks, or public recognition, or the satisfaction of knowing that the child is now well or the famine over. Universities are much involved in good desert: they hand out honorary degrees to the good, in recognition, as we say, of their services to the community. We also use the idea of desert in economic relations: the worker deserves a fair return for his labour, something, that is, which is proportional to what he has put into the job. Then there is ill desert; those who do wicked things, like Myra Hindley or Ian Brady, the Moors Murderers, deserve to be punished in proportion to the wickedness of their acts. Just retribution should be exacted. And when, regrettably, we see the wicked prosper, instead of suffering, we lament the fact that they have escaped their just deserts. Conversely when the good suffer, or indeed when anyone not conspicuously bad has a serious illness, or comes home to find their house burnt down, we lament the fact that fate has been cruel to them for they did not deserve what has happened. There is, we say gloomily, no justice in life.

Underlying all this talk of desert is a feeling that the good things and bad things that happen to people ought not to be simply the result of good luck, or bad luck, or devious cunning, but should make moral sense. Justice as desert is achieved when the good get their reward, and the labourer his due, and the wicked the appropriate punishment. The connection between this idea of justice and the law is obvious: law is a mechanism for bringing about such a state of justice, when nature has failed to do so unaided. So, for example, since murderers are often insufficiently punished by remorse, and are not regularly struck down by thunderbolts or bubonic plague, we have laws which make sure they are punished by imprisonment, or even death. Of course if you believe straightforwardly in heaven and hell things will always be put right in the next world, and it has always been a puzzle to explain why religious people still seem to want to jump the gun and punish on earth, though capital punishment could be viewed as a way of hurrying the sinner along to hell so that divine punishment will not be long delayed. Some Christian thinkers have indeed been puzzled by all this. I suppose a case might be made for saying that earthly punishment is really a kindness to evil-doers, as it will reduce the need for punishment in the afterlife. Every day in Wormwood Scrubs may mean one less day in the eternal fires, but as usually presented the deal seems a poor one.

The third basic idea involved in the notion of substantial justice is that of moral or, as it is sometimes called, natural *entitlement*. A just system of laws is one which distributes good things, of one kind or another, so that they are in the hands of those who are entitled to them, who have the best claim to them, who, as we often say, have a right to them. This overlaps with justice as desert, because people whose conduct is especially meritorious, like saving the drowning, may be felt to be entitled, because of their bravery, to some sort of reward. But the idea of justice as entitlement is capable of much wider extension than justice as desert, and as most people look at the matter does not deal with ill desert at all. Someone who is bad does not have a right to suffer or go to hell, though one philosopher, Hegel, has argued the contrary. It is a curious fact that some people who break the criminal law clearly want to be punished, perhaps because they feel that punishment somehow cancels their wrongdoing and wipes the slate clean. If you view punishment in this way then it becomes a good thing, and perhaps one to which one might be thought to have some sort of claim.

The theory of justice as moral or natural entitlement was developed by Aristotle and has been part of our way of thought ever since, though the association of it with individual rights is more modern. The difficulty with it has always been to settle the grounds upon which people are entitled to claim good things. There is also a difficulty in settling how far the theory ought to be taken. Should everything in life be distributed in a just way, or only some things?

So far as the first difficulty is concerned one view might be that everyone ought to have the same share of every good thing, just because they are human beings. But this seems both dreary and silly; what would be the point of everyone having a violin quite irrespective of any interest in playing one? And how depressing the world would be under such a sheep-like system. So all sorts of modified theories as to how things should be distributed have been offered – according to need, for example, or ability, or industry. Another idea is that what we need is a just system of distribution. For example, if we have three people and only two beds we might allocate the beds by drawing lots; this will not give all three the same thing, but we might accept such a system as involving a fair procedure, one that gave all three the same chance of getting a bed. A celebrated theory of this kind has been developed by the philosopher John Rawls.

In modern thought there has been much emphasis upon the idea that everyone is entitled at the least to a sort of minimum human happiness kit of certain basic rights, just because they are human. Britain has in fact subscribed to the European Convention on Human Rights, which embodies a considerable list of such rights. They fall into certain categories. Some are political, such as the right to free elections, freedom of assembly and association. Some are intellectual: a right to education, freedom of thought, freedom of expression, freedom of conscience and religion. Some deal with family life and privacy: freedom to marry, respect for family life and home, respect for private life and correspondence. Some deal with placing limits upon coercion: freedom from torture and degrading treatment or punishment, or slavery, the right to liberty and the right to a fair hearing. Strong theories of basic minimal rights involve the claim that they should never be violated, whatever the benefits this would bring to others. For example, torture should not be used even to compel a person who had hidden a nuclear bomb, ticking, in central London, to reveal where it is in time for the explosion to be prevented.

Such rights are sometimes called natural rights, and if this is taken seriously then attempts to say what they are, as in the European Convention, will not be viewed as conclusive. Statements of rights in consequence are looked at as merely 'declarations' of rights which people have anyway, by nature. A just system of laws will be one which ensures so far as possible that everyone gets these natural rights. So a system of law will be an unjust system if it fails to guarantee to everyone such rights as the right to education, to personal freedom of religion, to sufficient wealth to achieve a minimum standard of living above the poverty line, and so forth. Conversely a system which allows the rich to overeat, and the poor to starve, will be an unjust system, or as we often call it, an unfair system.

At the present time the language of rights has perhaps been used with an enthusiasm not matched by a practical concern to set up procedures which actually work and give people their rights. Britain, for example, has not even made the European Convention part of our law, which imposes great obstacles to its use by citizens. Indeed the world is littered with constitutions which guarantee various human rights, though little in the way of results follow from many of them. Furthermore rights are claimed which legal systems, even with the best will in the world, would find hard to deliver, such as a right to a job. The rhetoric of rights has perhaps got ahead of the reality.

So far as the second point is concerned, even the strongest believers in justice would agree that not everything needs to be justly distributed. If fifty people all fall in love with Marilyn Monroe justice is not a very useful concept to wheel out; for forty-nine of them life is going to be unjust, or as we would more normally put it, just tough. Perhaps one answer to this sort of problem is to be sought in just procedures; every suitor is entitled to put their case, but in this example the idea seems impractical and wrong, since it would invade the right to privacy. So we may have to limit the scope of any theory of justice as entitlement, and perhaps the world does not need an excess of justice.

Justice as *equality*, justice as *desert* and justice as *entitlement* are not mutually exclusive ideas; they will often interact with each other. But when we treat justice as a basis for critical consideration of the law and its doings, one or other of these three notions will usually be found to feature in the matter. Furthermore, as it always makes sense of a cooking recipe to ask if the end product is good to eat, so it always makes sense to ask of the law and its doings whether they are just, for, if we concede that social institutions should serve a purpose, the provision of justice seems to be a primary purpose of law. This does not however mean that the law may not have other aims and purposes, or that other purposes may not sometimes trump justice; for example, in tax law what is called there 'equity' (that is justice as equality) is sometimes subordinated to ease of collection. But it does mean that this aim is a particularly important one.

THE PROBLEM OF SOCIAL JUSTICE: FREEDOM AND EQUALITY

Today arguments about the justice of the legal system frequently turn on the idea of what is called social justice, that is a state of society in which a just distribution of good things is achieved. Many people believe that social justice is an aim which society should vigorously pursue through its laws. For example, it is often argued that government should intervene in the name of social justice to ensure that fair prices are charged for goods and services. They believe that high profits, called excessive profits, are something to which entrepreneurs are not entitled. If they make profits at all they should be reasonable ones. Again many people think that the state, through law, should establish educational systems designed to produce either equality of opportunity, or even equality of result. All children deserve an education which will iron out differences in social background and genetic make-up, and the law, it is claimed, should positively discourage or even do away with educational arrangements which do not fall in line. Again some argue that there should be 'positive discrimination' in favour of members of historically disadvantaged groups, a sort of reverse handicap system, in order to place them in a more equal position. It will be seen that the ideas of equality, desert and entitlement, particularly equality, feature prominently in our thinking on these matters.

These views are opposed by others who argue that greater social advantages are achieved by leaving more of the job of distribution to the operation of the free market, and who doubt either the wisdom or practicality of too enthusiastic a pursuit of egalitarianism through laws regulating education, or the fixing of prices. They favour an alternative method of distributing goods under the law: the free market. So long as people avoid fraud, coercion and trickery, and are not in a position of monopoly power, they should be allowed to buy and sell whatever they like, including their labour, or even their freedom, on whatever terms they like, and the law should uphold the contracts they make without troubling to enquire whether the result is fair or just or likely to favour a more egalitarian society. This line of argument is often linked to the claim that more freedom will lead to the production of more good things, or wealth, to be distributed, and in the end everyone will benefit. Supporters of the free market will of course wish to place some limits upon what may be bought and sold (most, though not all, would oppose a free market in babies), and they will also support fairness in the bargaining process. They support their case with a variety of arguments. For example, some emphasise the value of freedom as an end in itself, and view any interference with the right to buy education or whatever as an improper interference with freedom. Others may place more weight on the claim that in the long run the free market benefits everyone. Others may argue that the whole idea of a just distribution of good things in society is a vacuous notion, or that the idea of a fair profit, as distinct from a profit made by skill in making contracts in the free market, is empty of any meaning.

Controversy over the ideal of social justice and its compatibility with the free market often divides those of the political left and those of the political right, and in political argument there is usually much overstatement of the opposing cases. Behind the rhetoric lies the fact that although the free market economy may well lead to an increase in the stock of goods to be distributed and thus make it possible for everyone to be better off, and although it does bring with it an increase in freedom, it also seems to make possible very gross inequalities in the distribution of wealth. There is indeed a sense in which freedom (including freedom to buy and sell on any terms one likes) and justice (as equality, or as entitlement, or as desert) pull in different directions, and in a practical sense the problem is to balance the claims of one against the other.

THE RULE OF LAW AND THE PURSUIT OF FREEDOM

Homer in the Odyssey depicts the island upon which the Cyclops live as one where there is, outside the family, no society. Each monster lives in his individual cave, tending his herds of sheep and goats; there are no lonely Cyclops, since each cares nothing for his neighbours. Hence there are no laws, for none are needed; Homer calls laws 'judgements', not distinguishing between adjudication and law making, and thinking only of lawgivings. The implication of this tale, adapted for modern consumption, is that social life requires co-operation under order, and order requires laws. Otherwise the strong will simply grab what they want from the weak, and there will be no way of resolving disputes and conflicts, so as to enable co-operative social life to go on. This is of course no problem for the Cyclops, each of whom is self-sufficient, and apparently does not even engage in barter with other Cyclops. Homer does however remark that each Cyclops is a lawgiver and judge to his own children and wives, though quite how the matter of marriage was handled is not explained. Unless the Cyclops went in for incest, marriage would surely involve co-operation with other family groups. No doubt Homer based his Cyclops on the life of mountain shepherds whom you can find to this day in Greece living up on the mountains with the herds and having for long periods virtually no contact with anyone else. In this condition they need no laws.

Now we, who are not at all like Cyclops, could have

government, and perhaps order of a sort, by simply submitting to the rule of a leader, a dictator, or the members of a ruling elite, who were able to coerce the non-co-operative into obedience. One vision of the leader is of someone who is followed and obeyed blindly by his followers, even if they find his orders quite inexplicable. This sort of submission would be a pure case of submission to the government or rule of a man, or men. But such a submission to the rule of men could involve a loss of freedom which was worse than the disease it was supposed to cure, for it would subject the governed to the whims of the ruler, producing a state of unpredictability which was indeed not order at all. So those who value the order which is to be achieved through government and coercion, and also value freedom and pre-dictability, have tried to reconcile government with freedom, and the theory they have come up with is that of the rule of law. The solution they argue is the government of laws, not the government of men. F. A. Hayek, a modern expositor of this theory, puts it thus (*The Road to Serfdom* (1944), Chicago, 1976, p. 72):

Nothing distinguishes more clearly conditions in a free country from those in a country under arbitrary government than the observance in the former of the great principles known as the Rule of Law. Stripped of all technicalities, this means that government in all its actions is bound by rules fixed and announced beforehand – rules which make it possible to foresee with fair certainty how the authority will use its coercive powers in given circumstances and to plan one's individual affairs on the basis of that knowledge.

It will be seen how according to Hayek's argument the fact that government, which really means officials of one kind or another, are themselves controlled by law, protects citizens from arbitrary decisions and arbitrary coercion, and enables them to operate within the law and do their own thing. Another advantage of governing through rules will of course be efficiency; it is simpler to have rules (for example, saying what the cost of a television licence is) than individual commands, but this is not the point he wishes to emphasise.

The school I attended was not one much given, so far as prefects were concerned, to the rule of law, and what Hayek has in mind may be illustrated by the fate of a friend of mine, now a professor of theology. One night he was awoken from his sleep, and, without any explanation, savagely beaten with a cane. He retired to sleep again, as best he could, without ever enquiring why this had happened to him. His behaviour at first seems odd, but, in a world not governed by rules, was surely rational. Of what use was the information in a society where one could be so treated at the whim of a prefect, one in which their power was not controlled by any known rules? Suppose he had been punished because the bath water had run cold – next time it might be because it was too hot. It was better to remain silent, especially as even speech might provoke a further assault. Those who, like most of the readers of this book, have always lived in a relatively free society, in which the rule of law is to some degree followed out, may find it difficult to appreciate how different their lives have been from that of, for example, Jews in Hitler's Germany, where you simply never knew, when there was a knock on the door, what was going to happen next. There was a rule of law of a sort in Germany then, but it did not apply to Jews. Indeed one way of breaking down individual personality is to subject people to wholly arbitrary coercive control; this technique is used in early military training. The rule of law respects individual personality.

Those who believe in the rule of law concede that coercion is necessary to the production of order through law; at the same time they view the protection of personal freedom as a principal reason for wanting order. Coercion however seems the antithesis of freedom; they seek nevertheless to make coercion the friend of freedom by regulating its use, by confining it through rules of law. Now this alone cannot ensure that coercion is used only as a mechanism for freedom. For example, it was and probably is an offence in the army to engage in 'conduct prejudicial to good order and military discipline', and for this offence one was liable to punishment. Here indeed was a rule, but it was so vague that more or less anything could be covered by it; in practice, in my experience as a trainee, any whim of the hut corporal had to be obeyed for one to avoid being charged with this offence. So it was that we washed the coal, made our socks look square for kit-inspections, cut off the flowers of dandelions outside the hut with our table knives, polished the studs of our boots and collected the droppings of the Regimental Goat, Taffy V, from the parade ground. Laws as vague as this do not conform to the ideal of the rule of law. To put it another way, not any old law will do if you respect the rule of law. A topical example is section 2 of the Official Secrets Act, which is so widely drawn that it makes virtually any conversation with an official of any kind about their work a crime. Nobody is expected to take this seriously, but the law fails to give any real guidance as to what conduct is required for one to avoid falling foul of the authorities.

So it is that laws giving wide discretion, retrospective laws and secret laws are all incompatible with the rule of law. So too are laws which impose liability to punishment upon individuals who have not chosen to break the law, so that if we respect the ideal we can have no criminal liability imposed upon people who break the law by accident, or mistake, or on those who, because of mental deficiency, are not fully responsible for what they do. Again the rule of law will not be achieved if there are people to whom the law just does not apply; it requires that everybody must be subject to law. It also has a lot to say about legal procedures. It requires fairly and conscientiously conducted trials, because without them the law will cease to rule in the sense of dictating the outcome. If an innocent person is convicted and sent to prison, we have the rule of accident, not the rule of law.

So what may be called the spirit of the rule of law is capable of great elaboration, and can provide guidance both in the passing of laws and in their administration. So far as judges are concerned the ideal picture of a rule of law judge is of a person who takes decisions without paying any attention whatever to his own views and ideas and prejudices. He does what he does simply because that is the law, and there's an end to it. A straightforward example is of a judge sentencing a person who has just been convicted of murder by a jury. There is just one sentence, life imprisonment, and so a judge who sentences such a person to life imprisonment conforms perfectly to the rule of law. Of course if, as is common, he hurls a bit of abuse at the wretch *en passant* ('You monster you') then he departs from the ideal. There is no law telling him to do that, and some continental judges are very shocked by the English practice of dealing out impassioned abuse with the sentence, as in the case of the judge who once, albeit ludicrously, said: 'Not the least deplorable feature of these dreadful offences is that they took place beneath one of London's most beautiful bridges.'

The reconciliation between coercion and freedom can be carried one step further forward if the laws themselves are thought not to be the product of the whims of individuals. Thus according to democratic theory, though there are all sorts of difficulties with it, the laws are made by the people; the only limits upon their freedom are those they impose themselves. The most obvious catch here is the tendency of majorities to oppress minorities; one solution may be for the law to incorporate limits on the degree to which this can be done by entrenching certain freedoms, such as freedom of the press, as has been done under the US Constitution. Such constitutions limit the sorts of law which can be made so that legal mechanisms cannot be used to destroy the rule of law. So a constitution may forbid the passing of retrospective laws, or might, though I can think of no example, forbid the imposition of criminal liability without fault.

Lawyers come into the picture in two principal ways. As the people most directly involved in operating the legal system they are in a good position to make the reality of that system conform to the ideal; this is particularly true of judges. They also, through the practice of the law, help to make the law, and therefore the rule of law, actually available to people. There is no point having the rule of law but not letting people get at it. Thus those accused of serious crimes are commonly quite hopeless at presenting an adequate defence to a court. They are tongue-tied, frightened, unused to court procedures, ignorant of the rules that govern trials. Without legal counsel the rule of law is out of their grasp. So the spirit of the rule of law requires that the law should be accessible to citizens, though as we know it often is not. Institutions like the Citizens Advice Bureau are therefore the outworks of the rule of law. And since the function of the rule of law is to control official misconduct, it will be very important to have remedies which are actually effective in controlling them.

LAW AND ORDER

The ideal of justice looks towards a fair distribution of good things; that of the rule of law looks towards individual freedom as the goal, and claims that this can only be achieved by channelling coercion through the rule of law. Sometimes order achieved through law viewed simply as an end in itself is presented as a goal. This is the notion embodied in the catch-phrase 'Law and Order', a phrase which suggests that there is some natural connection between submission to law and an ordered society. As a political slogan 'Law and Order' has a powerful appeal. Imagine what would become of a political party which said it was opposed to 'Law and Order'. So it is that, especially at election times, there is competition in the political world to appropriate the phrase, and sell oneself as more likely to deliver 'Law and Order' if elected than the other party.

Devotees of law and order usually view the law, and more particularly its coercive agencies, principally the police, as an essential protection against the grosser forms of socially disruptive behaviour. So it is that law and order is contrasted with scenes of widespread rioting and violence, what are often called breakdowns in law and order. The staggering scale of shoplifting is not thought of as involving any such breakdown, though it would be if conducted by armed gangs who terrorised the supermarkets. Extensive street crime, involving violence or the fear of it, is another everyday example. The reduction in the sense of safety inhibits people in their daily lives. Obviously those who think that it is the law which normally produces order will have to concede that when riots occur there has been a failure to deliver the goods. At this point the law is viewed as an instrument by which order is re-established. In fact what happens when a riot is quelled is that this is achieved in the first instance by direct coercive force, by doing battle, as you can see on any newsreel of such an event. Trials and punishments come some time after the event, and usually affect only a tiny proportion of those involved. So what is meant here by law is force legitimated by law. With the business of applying coercion lawyers have only an indirect connection; the job is done by others.

Now one difficulty with the idea that law and order represents a distinct legal ideal is that order can be good or bad. So very evil regimes have been extremely orderly and well regulated. Many people therefore would only regard order as a means to an end, not an end in itself. The opposing view is that it is always better to live in an ordered society than in one that is anarchic. So, according to this view, although law and order does not get you very far, it at least gets you to first base; without it you can do nothing else. I suppose that this view makes more sense to those who, as in recent times in Cambodia or the Lebanon, have lived in anarchic conditions, than to those who have lived in peaceful Britain.

The second difficulty is that idealizing law and order suggests a connection between law and order which is probably false. In the village where I live, Wingham, there have been no riots in living memory. We sleepy Winghamites never feel the urge, and if we did would resist it on grounds of ethics, fear of social disapproval, or just idleness. When other mechanisms for producing order fail, as happened not long ago at Brixton, and at Mr Murdoch's print works in Wapping, the intervention of the agents of the law operates only as a temporary palliative, and indeed may make things worse; the gravest violence may be the official violence. So, it is argued, law may well be a vital last defence against individuals or small groups who disrupt society – for example, the Kray brothers or the Yorkshire Ripper. But in general order is not produced by the coercive mechanisms of the law. The happy condition of Wingham in general has nothing to do with the presence of our friendly village policeman, though everybody with children was glad to have him about when a child was brutally attacked recently in the village of Minster some few miles away.

Although confident views are often expressed on the matter, the truth is that we do not know a great deal about the connection between law and social order. The study of penology and criminology has been concerned to try to discover what effect criminal law and punishment have on people; huge quantities of research have been undertaken, but the results have been extremely modest. So arguments for and against the importance of criminal law in producing order may not be arguments about facts at all, but about competing ideologies, that is visions of the sort of world we live in. In any event it is not so much law as coercion which it seems, when matters become desperate, restores the peace. Those who elevate law and order into an ideal express a belief in the value of a homogeneous, disciplined society, and the achievements possible, as they think, in such a society. In terms of the ancient world they have a sneaking sympathy with Sparta, and, like the famous Victorian judge, James Fitzjames Stephen, they believe that coercion can be, and often has been, a force for good. They also, perhaps pessimistically, believe that human societies are essentially fragile, always at risk from subversives. Devotees of the rule of law, on the other hand, often view coercion as intrinsically evil; they tend also to be more optimistic in their view of human society – freedom and diversity will strengthen and not weaken human society, and it may be worth putting up with a certain amount of confusion in the process.

LEGAL ICONOCLASTS AND SORDID REALITIES

No sensible person has ever supposed that justice, the rule of law, and order, have ever been fully achieved by a legal system. To be sure there are people who talk ignorant rubbish about golden ages in the past, but no serious historian has ever come across one, and today the innocent are from time to time convicted, the evil do flourish, the good suffer, victims even of quite deliberate injuries are not compensated for them, and the use of coercive force to deliver law and order seems at times to be worse than the disease. Those who are committed to legal ideals can react to this lack of fit between the ideal and the actual in one of three ways.

The first is simply to admit that the law, like all other human institutions, is imperfect, and then try to do better. To this end many lawyers, like other citizens, take various forms of action designed, as they see it, to improve the law and its administration. In democratic societies this can be done through involvement in the world of party politics or in many other ways – by personal conduct, by joining pressure groups, by writing to the papers, by attempts to influence public opinion.

The second is to adopt the characteristic posture of the fearful ostrich, and simply refuse to accept that this lack of fit exists. This may show itself in behaviour; for example, the Court of Appeal, Criminal Division, and its predecessor, the Court of Criminal Appeal, has a perfectly terrible record of refusing to interfere in criminal convictions in situations in which nobody but an appeal judge would be confident that justice had been done. More commonly it shows itself in rhetoric. Thus at the time when the wisdom of retaining capital punishment was in debate the perfectly potty view was advanced that it was quite impossible, given the safeguards provided by law, for an innocent person *ever* to be hanged. One reason perhaps for such rhetoric is that it comforts those involved in taking terrible decisions to believe that they always get them right. The same phenomenon is commonplace in the memoirs of generals, whose errors send thousands to their deaths.

The third possible reaction is more radical, and goes beyond what might be called everyday rational scepticism. There is a long tradition in Western thought of the idea that law is essentially a mechanism for the preservation of inherently oppressive and unjust distributions of wealth and power in society. As such, law inhibits the development both of the individual and of the community. Remove oppression and injustice, and there would be no need for law, since order would exist without coercion. An illustration of this line of argument is the belief, once widely held, that crime is caused by poverty; if only we could eradicate poverty then there would cease to be a need for courts and prisons and policemen. It is an easy next step to argue that it is the pernicious and unjust distribution of wealth in society which causes poverty, and this distribution is preserved and protected by the law. So the law causes poverty and poverty causes crime; more simply, crime is caused by the law. A classic expression of this type of argument is Proudhon's epigram: 'Property is Theft.' Indeed much reasoning of this type has concentrated upon the institution of property, so central to the law, as the centre-piece in the argument. But a similar thesis can be developed in relation to the distribution of power, and many variants of the same sort of argument have been put forward.

Legal ideals can be fitted into this radical type of thesis by turning them on their head. The argument is as follows. A curious fact about the law is that its authority and objectivity are largely accepted by most citizens most of the time, and this even by people who seem to have nothing to lose by resistance except their chains. The legal system is viewed as morally legitimate; people believe they should obey the law even against their own self-interest. It is this acceptance which, as we have seen, makes recourse to coercion unnecessary most of the time. Radical sceptics treat legal ideals as sinister myths, whose function it is to help create a climate of opinion in which this spirit of docile submission will flourish. Thus, so the argument goes, the myth that law produces order in everyone's interests is used to legitimise baton charges by the police against strikers who would otherwise much improve their lot. The myth that judges, like the blind figure of justice, apply an objective existing body of law to disputes, without personal or political bias, serves to sell their decisions to the public. In short, ideals are there to hoodwink the oppressed.

An example of this theory applied to the notion of equality before the law is Anatole France's remark that 'The law, with its magnificent impartiality, forbids the rich as well as the poor from sleeping under the bridges of Paris.'

LEGAL THEORY AND THE RULE OF LAW

Battles between the sceptics and the idealists, though not under these names, have been going on now for centuries. At one time they centred on the idea of justice, some arguing that objective standards of justice, often called *natural law*, existed and were discoverable, whilst other doubted this claim. Today they centre rather more on the ideal of the rule of law. The subject which features in law courses as 'Jurisprudence', or sometimes 'Legal Philosophy', or 'Legal Theory', mainly consists in either defences of the ideal as both desirable and in principle attainable, or in claims that it is both pernicious, and impossible.

Much of the vast literature of jurisprudence centres upon the nature of judicial decisions. Here, if anywhere, official power in the hands of the judge should surely be ruled by the law. Now what the ideal of the rule of law seems to require is that decisions as to the rights and obligations, or guilt and innocence of citizens should be reached by the application of an objective body of rules, the law, to the facts of the case, so as to produce the decision which this process dictates. The court in this scheme of thought should serve merely as an instrument, a docile servant of the law.

Middle-of-the-road idealists claim that this is, quite regularly, the case. They concede that sometimes the judge may get the law wrong, and the judge or jury, if there is one, the facts wrong; there may be errors too in applying one to the other. But usually the job is done properly, just as on the whole civil aircraft are flown in the correct way, the pilots applying the proper rules and procedures to the situation which confronts them. But, they concede, this is not always so, not just because mistakes are made, but because there is ineradicable uncertainty as to what the law is or how it is to be applied. Laws are muzzy at the edges, and since this is so the personal choice of the judge of necessity comes into the matter. In the same way it is quite impossible in the nature of things to give pilots rule books to cover everything (a spitting cobra in the cockpit?) or to make the rules absolutely precise (cancel take-off if the co-pilot goes mad, but what does mad mean? And how mad?).

Wild idealists go much further: they argue that the law is capable in principle of providing one correct answer to every legal problem, though often human frailty is such that it will not be discovered. There are not many wild idealists about, but one, Professor Ronald Dworkin, keeps writing entertaining books and articles in favour of this position, even inventing a mythical super judge, called Hercules, who, it will be remembered, carried out jobs others thought impossible. Dworkin trys to explain how he manages to tease out of the legal materials the uniquely correct answer to the case before him. To make such an argument plausible it becomes necessary to develop a different concept of what being ruled by law means, which departs from the idea of being ruled by a rule.

Middle-of-the-road iconoclasts agree with middle-of-the-road idealists, but think that the muzzy area is more the norm than the exception, whilst wild sceptics may go to the point of claiming that the law cannot in principle ever determine the correct outcome of a case; hence cases are always determined by reasons other than the official ones.

Since much can be said on all sides of these arguments the series is likely to continue, and to some students of law at least the fascination of the subject lies in part in the fact that its study does raise fundamental issues of a philosophical character, issues which underly many of our attitudes to law, and which do not seem to have any obviously correct answer.

3

Legal Systems and Legal Traditions

One of the most important features of the civilization which developed in Western Europe is the profound significance accorded to law. Law defined the political organization and structure of society, provided a scheme of individual relationships within it, and contributed to the stability of society by offering an objective mechanism for the resolution of disputes and conflict within the community. The belief in the ideal of the rule of law is one of the consequences of this reverence for law. Another has been the conception of the ruler as the fountain of justice. Indeed for large periods in European history the two principal functions of government were thought to be the conduct of war and the administration of justice through law. Even today, when the functions of government have been extended to lengths undreamed of in past centuries, it remains true that government, at least on the surface, operates in internal affairs principally through legal forms and mechanisms, and even in international relations nations claim to act in accordance with the principles of international law, and conduct diplomacy in legal forms.

Now it is no doubt true that all extensive human societies possess law in some form or other, but it is certainly not the case that all societies attach the same central importance to legal forms and processes. Perhaps the most striking example of a successful society which for long periods did not do so is Imperial China, where, at a time when anti-legalism was at its height, recourse to law was thought so disgusting that both plaintiff and defendant in an action were soundly beaten before the case was heard to discourage such lamentable conduct in the future. Contempt for legalism as an aspect of Western decadence survived in Chairman Mao's China, where government was apparently conducted more through the influence of 'correct ideas', filtering down through the structure of the party, than through the promulgation of legal rules. Anti-legalism is currently in retreat in a China where they are busy trying to produce a corps of 500,000 lawyers to run their new society through law; it would be no surprise to see it revived. We tend to assume that legalism is a natural phenomenon everywhere; it is in fact a characteristic of only some forms of human association.

Where law has been valued, it has not always assumed the same form. Systems of legal thought, or, as they are often called, legal traditions, can be divided into groups or families. They are not coterminous with the boundaries of nation states, so that the same tradition can be in operation in what we view as a number of different countries, and within one country more than one tradition can be in force. Scholars have devised elaborate schemes for classifying legal traditions. Thus religious systems, such as Hindu or Islamic law, may, for example, be contrasted with secular systems, such as our own, which find their home in societies which have largely separated church and state. J. H. Wigmore, a celebrated American scholar, wrote a forgotten book on the subject which identified no less than sixteen such traditions; most scholars today would settle for a lower figure. However controversial some of these schemes are, most scholars would agree that Europe produced only two radically distinct professionalised legal traditions, which have, between them, spread over much of the globe. By far the older, for it goes back some centuries before Christ, is the Roman law tradition, also called, rather confusingly, the civil law tradition. It is so called because it was once the law concerned with the affairs of Roman citizens (Latin *cives* and hence civil). Its practitioners are consequently called civilians by the *cognoscenti*. Much younger is our common law tradition, developed in England in the course of the last 800 years or so, and having its roots ultimately in the pre-conquest world of Anglo-Saxon England.

A legal *tradition* is an aspect of general culture, and needs to be distinguished from a national *legal system*, meaning the body of rules in operation in a particular society at a given time, together with the institutions which go with them. Legal systems may be grouped into families according to the tradition to which they belong. Thus the Australian and New Zealand legal systems belong to the common law tradition, whilst the Italian and West German legal systems belong to the civil law tradition. Legal systems will usually be the property of a territorial nation state, for this has come to be the normal unit of political organization in the modern world. But legal systems can belong to other units of political organization, such as the European Community, based upon the Treaty of Rome. In the past, more than is the case today, legal systems were often conceived of as belonging to groups of people, rather than territorial states, and this idea of what are called personal laws (they belong to persons, not territories) is embodied in such expressions as 'The Law of the Medes and Persians, which altereth not', or, to give an early English example, the Law of the West Saxons. A modern example is the law of the Catholic Church, which applies to the faithful wherever they happen to be or live. In many Third World societies today a variety of bodies of customary law still apply to members of tribal groups, such as the Ashanti, living within larger territorial nation states, in this instance the modern state of Ghana, which is an artificial entity whose boundaries cut across tribal boundaries. Even our legal system allows people, within elaborate limits, to carry their law around with them like their spare clothing; a French honeymoon couple visiting England after a marriage in Paris do not start living in sin the moment they get off the boat at Dover. They carry their legal status as a married couple along with their luggage.

Legal systems do not emerge out of nothing; they possess a history, and reflect ideas, and make use of institutions, which have developed over time, and been moulded by cultural and political forces. The conceptions and categories employed in a legal system may be very modern; an example is that of 'unfair dismissal' in labour law, or 'capital gains tax' in taxation law. Or they may be fairly old, such as the conception of 'anticipatory breach of contract', which was invented in the nineteenth century. Or they may be of extreme antiquity, such as 'murder' or 'manslaughter', or the concept of a 'trust'. These conceptions are rarely invented out of the blue, by lawyers; usually, either now, or at some earlier time, they will have been in use as part of the stock of ideas existing outside the coterie of expert lawyers in the general culture of the society in which the system developed, or from which it was imported. The specialized ideas used by lawyers originate therefore in the everyday ideas of the society in which the law develops, though once they come to be refined by lawyers they tend both to fossilize and to become distinctively legal.

Since a nation's legal system, like its architecture or music, is a cultural phenomenon, the conception of a family of legal systems, or a legal tradition, involves grouping together particular legal systems which make use of the same basic ideas, and thus share some degree of cultural homogeneity. The fact that they do so is, of course, a product of history.

Legal systems in some ways resemble individual languages, and legal traditions are in some ways like the family groups into which we divide languages: Romance languages, like Italian and Spanish and Portuguese, which all share features derived from Latin, or Slav languages. Both legal systems and legal traditions also resemble languages in another respect: they provide schemes of categories into which the untidy business of life may be organized, and thought about. Languages enable us to communicate generally about life – tell stories, have family rows, give instructions. Legal systems and traditions have a more limited function; they are the means through which the special business of lawyers, which is the resolution of disputes and the ordering of social life through rules, can take place.

Across the frontiers of a particular legal system, but within the same legal tradition, there is mutual intelligibility. An English lawyer who moves to Canada (so long as he avoids Quebec which belongs to a different tradition) will not bring with him any detailed knowledge of Canadian law, be it provincial or federal, but he will have not the least difficulty in understanding Canadian legal materials, or in following an argument about Canadian law. Indeed, given very little homework, he can start to operate as a Canadian lawyer. But if he moves outside his own tradition, for example to Quebec, or to France, or to Iran, he will, as a lawyer, be quite radically lost and disorientated, and this even if his command of the French or Iranian language is generally perfect. He will find himself in a world in which the scheme of legal thought is quite alien to him.

The two legal traditions of Western Europe were developed in the medieval period, though the civil law tradition had, as we shall see, an earlier long history in the ancient world. Since medieval Europe largely shared a common Christian culture, and a common written language, Latin, it is somewhat surprising that it did not rest content with a single legal culture. But the English common law tradition, for reasons which are not fully understood, did, somehow, resist the pressure for uniformity.

EXPORTING LEGAL TRADITIONS

Legal traditions can spread around the world naturally, in the sense that nobody decides that this should happen, or be deliberately exported or imported. So far as the common law tradition is concerned, in relatively modern times it has been transposed to those many parts of the world which, at one time or other, lay within the area of British colonial and imperial influence. For example, Australia, Canada, most states of the USA, Ghana, Nigeria, Hong Kong and India, to mention but a selection, have all imported the common law or had it imposed upon them. Indeed one of the motivating beliefs of the imperial period was that Britain had a mission to bring the blessings of the common law to less fortunate peoples, an idea which now, in the period of post-colonial guilt, seems rather embarrassing. In many of those countries to which it was exported the common law was allowed to co-exist with other legal traditions, such as Hindu law in India, or Fanti or Ga customary law in Ghana. Part of the reason for this was the sheer difficulty in replacing local traditional law; another was a genuine respect for indigenous culture. Another factor was the theory of indirect colonial rule, which presupposed that indigenous institutions should in general be preserved. The common law has normally survived the break-up of the Empire. Indeed the survival of a common legal culture has been reflected in the fact that decisions of the English courts are still treated as an important source of law within some of the now independent Commonwealth countries.

The theory of the expansion of the common law was that in settled territories, where there existed no sophisticated indigenous body of law, as for example in Australia, the settlers took with them so much of the common law as was suited to their condition. This legal doctrine formalised what tended to happen anyway. In ceded or conquered lands, where an indigenous system existed, as in Nigeria or India, this indigenous law generally remained in force, except in so far as common law was deliberately introduced by Crown action or legislation. The theory did not happily accommodate the interests of indigenous peoples whose law was thought to be non-existent or un-developed, such as the Australian aborigines or the North American Indians, who of course got a pretty raw deal from the settlers. Some such peoples were allowed to keep their own system going within reservations; others were not. Today all over the common law world the question of the legal rights, usually land rights, of the original inhabitants, have become a much litigated area, and they have had some success in recovering rights which had been trampled upon in the process of European immigration.

In some countries which received the common law, such as the majority of the states in the USA, it has developed special characteristics, so as to create what may eventually become a wholly separate tradition, though this has not yet really happened; it is of course a matter of degree. Within the common law world, notwithstanding very various individual laws and procedures, there flourishes a common stock of ideas as to how law and legal systems should operate, how legal reasoning should be deployed and expressed, how lawyers and judges should behave and see their roles in society, as well as a common legal language in which legal ideas may be expressed. All this is lacking if you cross the boundary between common and civil law. I was once assured by a distinguished African lawyer from the Côte d'Ivoire, who had, of course, been deeply imbued with French culture, that he fully understood the problems of the English. They had no legal system, merely the fraudulent appearance of one, just as they possessed no *cuisine*, albeit they *ate things* of a nutritious but revolting character after processes that might be confused with cooking. He told me this in the kindly but confidential tones one might employ to tell a friend that he was suffering from bad breath, or had forgotten to insert his false teeth, and he was not joking. French lawyers do not joke much about law, any more than they do about so serious a matter as *la cuisine*.

THE CIVIL LAW TRADITION

Rome, so the story goes, was founded in 753 BC; the system of government was orginally monarchy or chieftaincy, and the early legal arrangements, about which we know nothing until the date of the early code known as The Twelve Tables of 451–450 BC, were the secret prerogative of the priests. Monarchy was followed by a Republic, and then by an Empire, which conventionally dates from 27 BC and the Augustan age. Most people, even if otherwise wholly ignorant on the subject, know that this Empire *Declined and Fell*, and believe this had something to do with sex. Never can a book title have so distorted understanding of history as the one Gibbon chose for his great work. For the striking fact about the Roman Empire was not that it declined and fell, though it did, but that it lasted a very long time indeed; compare it with the ephemeral British Empire, which ended almost as soon as it began. So in the west of Europe the Roman

Empire only lost its cohesion in the fifth century; in Britain, for example, the legions left in about 410 AD, and Romano-British culture, including Roman law, disappeared, leaving roads, ruins, town sites and place names but nothing besides. Elsewhere, as in the south of France, Roman culture never really disappeared at all. In the east of Europe the Empire survived until the fall of Byzantium (Constantinople, Istanbul) to the Ottoman Turks in 1453. So the Roman world in which Roman law operated was very long lasting.

From around 312 BC, when the priestly monopoly of secrecy was broken by a Roman equivalent of Clive Ponting, one Gnaius Flavius, until around 280 AD, Roman civilization developed an elaborate and very sophisticated body of private law, law that is which dealt with the relationship between citizens, rather than their relationship with the state. This private law was secular; its authority was not related in any way to a supposed divine or religious basis, but depended solely upon a claim to intrinsic rationality. The work of developing this body of law was undertaken neither by state officials, nor by legislators, nor by judges, nor by barristers, nor even by law professors, but by jurists, a class of men who usurped from the priests the role of legal expert. One of them was so revered that the Senate gave him a free house on the Appian Way where he could more easily be consulted; he was known, like the pugilist Muhammad Ali, as 'The Greatest'. It is hard to imagine a lawyer today achieving such status, and the story indicates how exalted a place law occupied in Roman thought.

Jurists have no real equivalent in modern society. We may start from saying what they were not. They were not judges; that job was done by laymen, who were chosen by the parties to the case to act as judges. The judges were expected to apply the law of the jurists to decide the issue in dispute, which was put in the form of a question formulated by a state official known as the Praetor. Nor were they advocates who, like Cicero, made speeches in court; jurists thought advocates to be a pretty scurrilous lot, prepared to talk any nonsense for their clients. Jurists instead were wealthy patrician individuals who acted not as court lawyers, but as legal consultants, and wrote books about the law, not in return for money, but simply to acquire honour and prestige in a society which revered law. Some were also active in public life generally, for example the jurist Ulpian, who was Prefect in York early in the third century. Poor Ulpian came to a sticky end, being eventually murdered by the Praetorian Guard, in 223 AD, but when not involved in the dangerous world of politics he wrote law books, and his legal opinions, or some of them, have lived on, as have some of the works of other jurists, such as two others who are known to have visited Britain: Papinian (also murdered rather earlier, in 212 AD) and Paul, who lived at around the same time. There were very many other jurists, such as Sabinus, who founded what was known as the Sabinian school, probably a school of thought, and his rival, one Proculus.

The survival of parts of what was once a huge body of juristic literature took place in a curious way. Juristic opinions were expressed in various literary forms, such as collections of *responsa* (answers to questions), or commentaries on statutes, or on other jurists' writings, and with very rare exceptions the texts of almost all of these works have been lost. But extracts from them have survived through the codification of law decreed early in the sixth century by the Emperor Justinian of Byzantium, a codification which produced what is called the *Corpus Iuris Civilis*, which we may translate as *The Compendium of Civil Law*.

Justinian, a boorish creature, whose picture in mosaics you can still see in Ravenna, was trying to restore his prestige after having been nearly toppled in an outbreak of hooliganism by gangs of chariot-racing supporters. Egged on by his wife Theodora, a tough-minded former prostitute, he cancelled plans for a swift departure from his capital and, having first had killed 30,000 or so of the hooligans, he set about restoring himself through prestige projects. One project, and you can still see the result, involved grandiose architecture. He had built the great Church of St Sophia, familiar even to the architecturally un-educated through the James Bond film *From Russia with Love*; the first attempt to build the vast dome failed when it fell down, but a new version has been around ever since; later a mosque, it is now in effect simply a museum. Justinian's other prestige project was legal. He established a commission to codify the laws, which were to be found in the massive body of surviving juristic writing. The job, under the direction of a remarkable man called Tribonian, was completed with amazing rapidity by 534 AD In addition to a collection of statutes (called the *Codex*) it comprised a *Digest* and a book of *Institutes*. The *Digest*, a work of around 800,000 words, was a compendium of juristic law, roughly sorted out into topics. This was formed by the paste and scissors method; that is to say it consists entirely of quotations from the ancient jurists, as it were stuck together to form a legal code. These quotations were, however, doctored, with the aim of ironing out any inconsistencies and obscurities, an aim not in fact achieved; unhappily we are not told what alterations were made, and have so far as possible to guess.

A passage from it reads like this:

Pomponius in his ninth book commenting on Sabinus. Sabinus gave it as his opinion that if I order some object, such as a statue or vessel or garment, to be made for me in return for my giving simply money, this is held to be a sale, and that there cannot be a hiring where the material is not supplied by him for whom the object is made. The result would be different if I supplied a site for you to build a housing block on, for in that case the principal thing comes from me.

It will be seen from this example that it is possible to derive a general principle, or perhaps two principles, as to the distinction between two legal categories, *sale* and *hire*, from this text, and an ingenious mind can soon invent hypothetical cases falling on the borderline. For example, suppose a dentist is employed to fill a tooth, he providing the gold for the filling – is this a sale, or a hiring of services? Of course this will only matter if the law of sale differs from the law of hire, as was long the case in English law, for contracts for the sale of goods worth more than ten pounds required written evidence, whereas contracts of hire did not.

The use of doctored quotations seems a bizarre way of carrying out the enterprise of codifying a legal system; today we would try to reproduce the substance of the juristic law in contemporary and concise language. But the method used reflected a belief that the ancient jurists of the late Republic and early Empire belonged to a lost legal golden age. By retaining their very words, so far as possible, the work of Justinian's compilers could be purveyed as carrying their personal authority.

The *Institutes* was an official first-year comprehensive textbook on private law for students in the law schools of Byzantium and Beirut; it also was given legislative force, so the book from which they learnt about the law was itself the law. It was based on an earlier such work by a very obscure jurist called Gaius, who was probably a law teacher. Gaius' *Institutes*, originally a set of lecture notes, dates from about 150 AD. It is the only more or less complete legal work from the golden age (called the classical period) which has survived untampered with by Tribonian's codifiers; a nearly complete manuscript turned up in Verona in 1816, and some fragments have been found elsewhere since.

In Western Europe Roman law survived as a living system in some areas, such as Italy, even after the administrative collapse of the Empire, but not, as we have seen, in others, such as Britain. But in the Dark Ages direct knowlege of the old texts themselves faded, and they themselves were lost. In the East forms of Roman law remained in force even after the collapse of the Empire in 1453, for example in Greece, in a shadowy way, until this century. By good fortune, however, two manuscripts of Justinian's codification survived in Italy, and were rediscovered in the twelfth century. To people of the time, deeply impressed by the physical relics of high Roman civilization which they could see around them, these old texts revealed legal skills greater than any they seemed to possess. So communities of teachers and students grew up in north Italy, especially at Bologna, to read and expound the ancient juristic texts. Students hired teachers, and flocked from all over Europe to their lectures; that indeed is how universities as we know them originated. Bologna rapidly became an international legal centre, with over 10,000 students, far larger than any modern law school, and other universities were established, as in Paris, Oxford and even Cambridge, in which the teachers, not the students, were in control. Studies in these law schools naturally centred upon the exposition of the ancient texts – they could be explained, commented upon and sorted out into better schemes of arrangement. Inconsistencies could be spotted and ironed out, and hypothetical problems solved by arguments based upon them. So Roman law study became primarily a matter of textual interpretation and exposition.

Students who had taken law courses moved into positions of importance in government, the church and judicial administration. They took with them the ideas they had acquired at law school, just as they do today. The consequence was that the multifarious customary legal systems of Europe, which differed from place to place, and person to person, came to be re-interpreted, and indeed submerged, by notions derived, albeit in a roundabout way, from the ancient texts. At the same time the law became more uniform. This process, which happened in different ways in different places, is called *The Reception*; it profoundly affected most European countries. France, for example, once governed by hundreds of different bodies of customary law, such as the Custom of Paris and the Custom of Orleans, came to have just French law, and that was highly derivative of Roman law. The Western church, a sort of super state, also came to be dominated by legally trained graduates, and that is why perhaps it seems today sometimes so legalistic in its attitudes. Employing modes of thought derived from the civil law churchmen developed the law of the Western church, which is called canon law, and this applied throughout Christendom to matters which fell within the church's jurisdiction, for example to the institution of marriage. The whole process of the reception was inspired by the belief that the ancient texts, properly understood of course, set out intrinsically rational solutions to the problems of human relationships; they were called 'written reason'. It was belief in their intellectual force which carried the day.

This, in bare outline, is how Europe, England apart, came to evolve a common legal culture. Indeed Roman law was called *ius commune*, the common law of Europe, just to confuse us, for we like to confine the use of the term common law to English law.

HISTORICAL ORIGINS OF THE COMMON LAW

Our legal system, from which the common law tradition is derived, developed quite differently; it did not take its origin from a text of any kind, but from tradition expressed in action. It began as the customary law used in the court of the king when the court was settling those disputes and conflicts which were thought to concern the monarch directly. Originally these included only the graver crimes (called pleas of the Crown) which were thought to disturb the monarch's tranquillity, the royal 'peace', and property and other disputes involving the king's immediate feudal tenants. Norman feudalism was essentially a military system, and as leader the king had to keep the peace between his men, and this he did in his court. There were many other courts in England, all administering their own customs. There were feudal courts run by lesser lords for their tenants, and courts in manors, and special courts for villeins. The royal hunting forests all had special courts administering the forest law, and the miners of Devon and Cornwall ran their own stannary courts. There were courts in the counties and the hundreds and the boroughs, and soon the universities, and the church ran its own elaborate system to deal with spiritual matters through the canon law. So there was much diversity of law, law meaning traditional custom.

The royal court means not a building but the royal entourage, and as well as cooks and carvers and fools and chaplains this included some clerks or clerics, that is churchmen who were literate, the church being in the forefront of the high technology of the time. By Henry II's time, and he reigned from 1154 to 1189, some of them were *specializing* in legal business and acting as deputies for the King in the administration of justice. As such they had royal authority, being substitutes for the king. For that reason if you killed a High Court judge when acting as a judge that was treason, for which you could be hanged, drawn and quartered, not mere murder, for you would have killed someone who stood in the very shoes of the monarch, and killing monarchs is treason, not murder. These clerks had power to judge, power over litigants, not merely power derived from the litigants' consent. They were neither arbitrators, nor umpires, nor mediators; they were judges.

As bureacrats everywhere do, they established formalised procedures for hearing disputes, and these used standardised written documents, just like the forms used today to apply for a passport or enter a university. In particular they used writs, formal documents issued in the king's name, to start actions and initiate procedural steps in them, such as summoning juries. Soon they began to keep what we would call files; they used writing to compile vellum rolls to record the formal steps in the case and its outcome. Their practices, essentially preserved as an oral tradition, formed the common law of England, the law which was available, throughout the realm, to everyone to whom it applied. It was common as a prostitute is common: available to all. Under Henry II one of these clerks, whose name we do not know for certain, was inspired to write a book about these practices. This book is called Glanvill's *Treatise on the Law and Custom of England* though Ranulf de Glanvill, a senior royal judge, did not actually write it; perhaps he sponsored it. The author explained what it was intended as an *aide-mémoire*, which might be useful, though incomplete, in setting out the practices followed, and the text of many of the documents used. He explained that it was quite impossible in his time for anyone to write a complete account of all the laws in force in the Realm of England; nobody who could write could possibly know what they all were. His was a modest undertaking, but nothing comparable could have been produced anywhere else in Europe at this time.

The fact that the royal customary common law was well established, backed by a powerful monarchy and in the hands of literate experts *before* the revival of Roman law studies may be the principal explanation for English resistance to the reception of Roman law.

Over the following centuries certain critical developments both extended the scope of the common law system, and altered its character. Originally this extension only meant that it became available everywhere in the realm, and not simply where the travelling king's court happened to be at any particular moment. Through the sending of judges around the country, as mobile libraries and blood transfusion clinics travel around today, common law became ubiquitous. In the course of time the extension of royal justice took on another aspect: it began to swamp and supersede the activities of other courts. The royal deputies not only claimed the power to say what the bounds of other jurisdictions were. They also usurped jurisdiction, that is they stole cases from other courts, perhaps because litigants wanted royal justice, perhaps because the judges, being paid from fees, made money out of doing so. So the common law jurisdiction expanded, and the jurisdiction of other courts accordingly diminished.

This process of extension took place over many centuries. For example, the common law only took over disputes arising out of verbal contracts on any great scale in the sixteenth century, whilst jurisdiction over marriage cases came over in the nineteenth century. Many other courts, applying other bodies of law, survived until quite modern times, like the civil court of the University of Oxford, in which the late Harold Macmillan was once sued for a tailor's bill. Some few still do. But the general movement was all one way, until quite modern times. All of this had the result of making the common law seem to be the national law, the law of the land as we say, and this is how common lawyers today view the system. In modern times the process has to a considerable degree been reversed by the development of a large range of tribunals outside the common law system, and by the acquisition by civil servants of extensive adjudicative functions. But we still tend to think of the common law system as the only system.

This progressive expansion of the common law was achieved without a massive increase in judicial staff by the use of justices of the peace to conduct a mass of criminal and administrative business, and by the use of the jury of local laymen to share the work of adjudication. Juries came to be the typical trial mechanism once more mysterious mechanisms, which relied on divine involvement, like ordeals and battles, had disapppeared. The small coterie of expert lawyers looked after the law, whilst the unpaid laymen, of whom there was an inexhaustible supply, were drafted in to deal with the facts. Until the nineteenth century there were usually only a dozen professional common law judges, known as the twelve men of scarlet; only in very recent times, with the eclipse of the jury in civil cases, has the number of professional judges risen sharply.

The character of the system changed in two critical ways. One involved secularisation: the common law separated from the church. Originally the legal experts were in church orders, the church alone being able to provide the bureaucractic skill of literacy. But by around 1300 a small profession of court lawyers had evolved, the only literate yet lay profession in Europe. In the fourteenth century the judges came to be appointed from these court lawyers. In time they developed their own systems of education, mirroring university practices, but operating outside them, and organizing themselves in the fraternity houses in London called Inns of Court. The evolution of a separate educational system also insulated the common law from the civil law, which was studied in the two universities of Oxford and Cambridge where clerics were educated, but not in the Inns of Court in London, where, in the words of the poet Spenser, the studious lawyers have their bowers. The Inns came to be viewed as a university of the common law, and there was no rival university in London to contend with.

The second was that the judges, instead of confining themselves merely to regulating the *procedures* whereby cases were handled, began to exercise control over the *substance* of how the cases were determined. When cases were resolved by God's intervention, and this was the theory underlying trial by ordeal, by battle, or by oath swearing, this would have been presumptuous and absurd. But once juries came in the experts could hardly fail to feel that they might know better than the laymen, called in the Norman French of the time, *les lay gents*, what standards to apply to decide the dispute. So the judges took what is, as we have seen, the critical step of moving from controlling mere procedure into developing what we call substantive law.

This was brought about through the elaboration of what is known as special pleading, a process of allegation and counter-allegation designed to settle what the dispute is all about before it is tried. Pleading can be general. For example, in a criminal court dealing with a murder the prosecution will allege that the accused murdered someone and the accused will either agree (by plea of guilty) or disagree by pleading that he is not guilty. The plea here is general: it generally denies the accusation and does not narrow down what the dispute is about. For example, the accused may claim that the person died naturally, but the plea does not reveal this. Special pleading, which was evolved mainly in civil law, does have this narrowing function. Using the same example, a special plea might confess that the accused had deliberately killed the victim, but try to avoid the legal result by adding that the accused was an executioner and the victim had been sentenced to death. If the prosecution say by their reply that this is all rubbish we have narrowed the issue down before it goes for trial. In civil cases, but only to a very limited degree in criminal cases, the courts evolved the system of special pleading, designed to determine precisely what the dispute was all about before it was submitted to the jury for determination, and this was elaborated to differentiate what were called questions of fact, which were for the jury to decide, from questions of law, which were for the expert judges to decide. Through deciding such questions the judges could build up official expert views as to the substantive principles to govern the decision of litigated questions. So substantive law evolved as a mechanism for controlling the free discretion of juries to act as people's courts.

Suppose, for example, that two people have made a contract, and one is refusing to perform it because, as he claims, it has become impossible to do so. Should he still pay damages? The whole matter can just be left to the jurymen to decide; if so we shall have a decision, but the case will generate no legal rule as to the relevance of impossibility as a defence to a breach of contract. All we shall have is a jury decision one way or the other, and nobody but the jurymen will know why it was given. Instead suppose that the defendant is allowed to concede, by a special plea, that he did not perform, but add that performance had become impossible. The plaintiff may agree that this is what happened, but say in his reply to the special plea that in his view this should not provide any defence. We have now by pleading, by allegation and counter-allegation, isolated the abstract question 'Is impossibility a defence to an action for breach of contract?' This has become what the dispute is all about, and we can now hand this question over to the expert judges to decide. In effect the system of pleading has created a distinction between matters of law, matters to be settled by expert opinion, and questions of fact, to be settled by lay common sense.

For the common lawyer substantive law consists in the way in which such questions are answered by the judges in accordance with expert tradition. The creation of substantive common law setting out people's rights and duties and obligations, and creating structures of responsibility and excuses and justifications and defences, simply consists of this take-over by the lawyers of questions which otherwise would be settled by uninstructed common sense. Various other procedural mechanisms were in time evolved to express and create the distinction between law and fact, but it appears to have principally originated in the way I have explained.

CENTRAL CHARACTERISTICS OF THE COMMON LAW

No two writers would be likely to agree on a list of the characteristics of the common law tradition, but few would disagree on one, which is its casuistic character. Whereas the foundation for law to a civil lawyer is a *text*, to a common lawyer

70

it is a *case*, and this remains true even when a common lawyer is dealing with a statute. His interest is not so much in what the statute says, but in what courts have or may make of it. The centrality of the case has always been typical. When, centuries ago, Geoffrey Chaucer was trying to give a picture of a lawyer, the Serjeant at Law of the Canterbury Tales, he equips him with only one sort of hardware:

> In bookes had he cas and doomes alle,
> That from the tyme of King Wylliam hadde yfalle.

In more recent time we have the poem about Old Father William, in which he reports of himself that in his youth:

> I took to the law,
> And argued each case with his wife,
> And the muscular strength which it gave to my jaw,
> Has lasted the rest of my life.

Nothing here has changed, and today the study of law throughout the common law world centres upon the study and analysis of tens of thousands of cases, slices of real life, which have come before the courts for decision, and dissection of the way they have been decided by the judges. In America a whole system of legal education, the case method, shown in the movie *Paperchase*, centres upon the idea of the leading case, from which may be teased out the deep principles of the law. Much of both the fun of legal education, and its intellectual interest, stems from the bizarre stories which come before the courts in litigation, and the fascination in trying to reach rationally defensible conclusions as to what should be done about them.

Take for example the case where the smallest dwarf in England was trodden on by the largest elephant, Bullu, a creature of the highest character, whilst working in a circus into which had been introduced, wrongly, a Pomeranian dog, whose presence upset Bullu. Indeed he panicked. Should the circus proprietor pay up? Or the case in which a melancholic judge casts himself into the River Stour at Canterbury at a time when it was the law that anyone who committed felonious homicide *in his lifetime* forfeited his property to the Crown; has the judge committed the felony *in his lifetime*? Or only *after his death*? This was a sixteenth-century case which amused Shakespeare; it really happened, and involved the Canterbury family of Hales, who were forever drowning themselves, as you may see from a memorial in the cathedral there. Or take this American case: a person is, through the negligence of one individual, falling to certain death and is, *en passant* as it were, electrocuted through the negligence of someone else. Who caused the death? Who pays? Suppose that at a pheasant shoot you are able to show that one of two people peppered you with shot, but you cannot prove which, and they keep their mouths shut. Should they share the bill for medical expenses, or should your action for damages fail upon the ground that you have failed to show that either of them did the deed? Or take the case of a will whereby property is left to someone so long as they are 'adherent to the doctrines of the Church of England'. What on earth are the doctrines of the Church of England? Is there any way of telling, and is not the obscurity surrounding them the chief glory of the Anglican church? And how do you show that you are adherent to them? Criminal law abounds with strange tales. If an intending Colchester rapist, having obtained a ladder, and removed all his clothing except his socks, climbs up to a lady's bedroom window with criminal intentions but is then, to his amazement, welcomed with open arms by his intended victim, who mistakes him for her boyfriend (who regularly arrives in this manner), can he be convicted of burglary? If two very hungry sailors, in the aftermath of a shipwreck, kill and eat a ship's boy, who is on the verge of death anyway, is that murder? Or just good nutritional sense? If a person dishonestly votes in an election in the name of someone who is dead, can he be convicted of the statutory offence of 'personating a person entitled to vote', for the dead are surely not entitled to vote? Is a prostitute waving from a window above a street guilty of the offence of soliciting *in* the street? If she is not soliciting *in* the street how is it that people in the street are being solicited? The common lawyer sees the law as starting from decisions in tricky cases such as these; law consists of the principles according to which these cases have and ought to be determined, and these principles are thought to have no uniquely correct verbal form. The common law is not a text, and there is a sense in which, because it is always on the move from case to case, you never quite know from case to case what it is.

The casuistic character of the common law has meant that it has evolved practically in response to immediate problems, not theoretically, away from the scene of action. It is rich in detail, and somewhat weak in general principles. In the past it has evolved largely in courts, not in universities as has been the position in civil law jurisdictions. Indeed until quite recent times it was not studied in universities in England at all. After the decline of the system of education in the medieval Inns of Court it was learnt and transmitted largely through a system of practical if tedious apprenticeship. A consequence of this has been its theoretical poverty and highly disorderly character. Its highest intellectual achievement, the law of property in land, was described by Oliver Cromwell as an ungodly jumble, and with some justification.

In the last century-and-a-half, largely through the work of systematising writers on the law who, in modern times, have tended to work as university scholars, it has become more orderly, but it still at times retains an air of amateurish muddle, or so at least it would seem to a civil lawyer. Hand in hand with lack of system has gone vagueness; common law, unlike a good lettuce, is never crisp. As it has evolved case by case so the common law is court-centred; its acolytes are the court lawyers, the barristers, and the high priests of the system are the judges, the oracles of the law, traditionally supposed to carry the law in their bosoms. Drawn in England from the argumentative barristers, they carry on to the bench the characteristics which have led to success at the bar. Some of these qualities are not admirable: at worst they may include bumptious self-confidence, vanity, egocentricity and an inability to think in general terms about the working of the law in society. At best common law judges possess remarkable fluency in expression, masterful ability in analysing complex bodies of information and a firm grasp of the workable. The virtues and vices of the English bench simply mirror those of the bar, and the same may perhaps be said of the common law itself.

THE HISTORICAL CHARACTER OF THE LAW

A system of law which has, as it were, grown up, rather than been laid down, is bound in the nature of things to be wedded to tradition, to the idea that what should be done now is what has been done in the past. Without a commitment to tradition the law would indeed be nothing more than a wilderness of single instances. The formal expression of this traditionalism is called the doctrine of precedent, and it has been much elaborated by lawyers and theorists. It says that decisions in past cases should govern present cases which exhibit no relevant differences from them, unless the result looks quite absurd. Respect for precedent can be valued as giving stability to the law, or as objectifying the law as something beyond the whim of the individual judge, or as leading to justice through equal treatment before the law. A duty to respect precedents can also be combined with the recognition of a pecking order of courts: lower courts must accept and follow precedents set by higher courts, and this is indeed how the system works.

All this might seem to imprison the law in a rigid conservative straitjacket, for in so far as precedents are respected, law at any given period might seem to become a mere product of ancient history. But even in very conservative epochs this has never been entirely the case. However conscientiously they are respected precedents always leave much room for argument. For example, earlier cases are only supposed to govern later cases where the situation is a similar one in all relevant respects. This can, as we have seen, be controversial. Thus lawyers can argue as to whether the case law governing liability for the bad behaviour of one's dogs should govern liability for the independent torts of one's cats. Are cats, in all relevant respects, like dogs? The leading case on this entertaining subject inspired a celebrated judicial opinion which includes the remarkable statement: 'My Lords, I can see no difference between a dog and a cat.' Again there can be great obscurity as to what exactly an earlier case did decide about the law. A famous modern decision on the law of murder, *Director of Public Prosecutions* v. *Smith*, falls into this category, so appallingly badly written was the judicial opinion in the case.

These problems are more or less inevitable, inherent that is in a precedent-based system. But a respect for precedent is in continual conflict, with two competing ideas to which lawyers are also committed in varying degrees. One is that as the world changes, both materially and with respect to beliefs and attitudes, so should the law change. The other is that the mere fact that something has been done in the past does not seem, by itself, to ensure that what was done is rationally defensible; perhaps what was done in the past was silly then and still silly now. Surely legal decisions should be rationally defensible? Plainly these ideas can be at odds with respect for precedent. This raises another difficulty. If we value respect for precedent as a way of ensuring that judges are bound by law, and do not just make it up, making the law rational and up to date seems to involve some impropriety. So judges who try to be rational and up to date may appear to some to be playing fast and loose with the ideal of the rule of law.

Nobody has ever really resolved these apparent contradictions in our conception of the nature of the judicial process and its relation to the rule of law, though they have tried for centuries. In consequence a vast literature of a philosophical character, to which I have already referred, grapples inconclusively with the theory of judicial decision. One traditional way out of the difficulties involved is to say that the law consists in deep principles of rationality *underlying* the cases. These deep principles remain constant over time, though their correct application may change as the world changes, or as their true import comes to be better understood. Precedents are only valuable as illustrating these deep principles, and if they fail to reflect them correctly then they have no force. Sceptics on the other hand doubt if these supposed deep principles are more than myths. To the sceptic they resemble such propositions as that 'God moves in a mysterious way', whose function, a sceptic might claim, is to reconcile our essentially contradictory beliefs about the Deity – that He is both All Good, and at the same time All Powerful – both with each other, and with the horrors of the world we inhabit and He, according to another belief, made.

LAW AND EQUITY

A legal system indeed is doomed to grapple with contradictions: it needs perpetually to attempt to reconcile demands which are in conflict with each other. It must be a force for stability, yet at the same time it must be adaptable, and capable of change as society changes. It must, if it is a legal system at all, operate through general rules, yet it must be prepared to make exceptions to general rules when a slavish conformity to them would produce an unjust or indefensible result, or when some gap in the rules can be exploited to produce absurdity. The common law system reacted to these needs in a very peculiar way, by the development, alongside the courts of Common Pleas, King's Bench and Exchequer, which all administered *common law*, an entirely different court, the Court of Chancery, which administered not law, but something quite different called *equity*. Today we might expect at least some of the problems which generated this arrangement to be handled by parliamentary legislation, but in earlier times this was not the mechanism used, and even today legislation is not promoted on a scale which copes adequately with them.

To lawyers brought up in the civil law tradition this division between law on the one hand and equity on the other is perhaps the weirdest feature of our legal system. How it all began is still not entirely clear, and perhaps never will be. So what follows is at best merely an attempt to explain the matter.

By the early fifteenth century the system of common law was very fully developed; the law was passed down essentially as an oral tradition amongst a very small legal profession, consisting effectively of about a dozen judges, about the same number of serjeants at law, and perhaps forty or so important barristers and court officials. What these people thought to be the law, was the law. They lived and worked together, forming a cohesive group, and were understandably conservative in their approach to the job. Stability and the rule of law, not of discretionary justice, was what they valued.

The system they operated was however defective. There were individuals who for one reason or another did not think that the system was providing them with justice, and after all that was what the system was supposed to deliver. One remedy they had was to petition the king, as fountain of justice, setting out their complaints, just as today people write to the Lord Chancellor when they think a magistrates' court or a circuit judge has not given them justice. The King, whose powers were nowhere set down, or his Council, might do something to help them. In the fifteenth century the practice developed of referring these petitions to the Lord Chancellor, who was the King's principle minister and head of his secretariat, instead of their being considered by the monarch himself or the Royal Council. By about 1450 or so the Chancellor himself was dealing with a large number of such petitions and making orders on his own authority. His authority probably depended upon the terms under which he had been appointed, and was derivative of the royal authority. These orders were called decrees, and they provided petitioners with a remedy when the common law did not do so.

For example, the common law courts did not recognize what we would call trusts. Someone might decide to transfer landed property to two trusted friends of his, with instructions that they were to look after the property, not for their own benefit, but for the benefit of his infant son; he trusted them to carry out his wishes. Such a transaction might make sense, for example, if the property owner was off to the battle of Agincourt, and knew he might not return. The common law courts took the view that since the ownership had been given to the two friends, they alone had legal rights in the property. Hence if they misbehaved and broke the trust reposed in them there was nothing the law could do about it; the law dealt in legal rights, not trusts. The son, if eventually cheated out of lands which his father wished him to enjoy, could however petition the Chancellor to do him justice. The Chancellor would then examine the two faithless friends, the trustees as we would call them, and make a decree ordering the faithless friends to carry out the trust reposed in them, on pain of imprisonment if they failed to do so. As well as enforcing trusts the fifteenth-century Chancellors developed a practice of intervention in other types of case: for example, they would order the specific enforcement of contracts to convey land, whereas the common law only gave damages, and they would intervene where there had been fraud or mistake in formal transactions. So the practice of the Chancellor was supplementing the common law and remedying some of its imperfections.

The medieval Chancellors apparently had a theory under which they intervened, and one which provided an intellectual justification for their activities. They were always churchmen, holding bishoprics and other eccesiastical positions of profit, but they were also nearly always lawyers, having taken degrees in civil (that is Roman) law and canon law at Oxford or Cambridge. Those that were not were theology graduates, who also knew about the canon law. Obviously they could not claim to be administering either common law (for that was the business of the common law judges) or civil or canon law. Civil law was not in force in England, and canon law was the business of the church courts. So they developed the idea that they were not administering law of any kind; instead they claimed to be administering *conscience*, and what this meant was that they were insisting that legal rights should be exercised in accordance with good conscience, that is in a way which was not sinful. Conscience was the faculty which human beings possessed which kept them from risk of hell-fire, though in tricky borderline cases, cases of conscience as they were called, they might need professional advice from expert confessors. The

Chancellors, according to this theory, were not in any way seeking to undermine legal rights, but they were recognizing that legal rights can be abused in sinful ways. In our example the two friends have the legal rights in the property, but they are seeking to abuse these rights in a way which a well-directed conscience would see was wicked and sinful. The Chancellor's order to honour the trust placed in them merely keeps them on the straight and narrow and preserves their souls from damnation. So it was that in the fifteenth and early sixteenth centuries the Chancellor's court was usually called a court of conscience, not a court of equity, much less a court of law.

A modern analogy may make the idea of the institutionalised distinction between law and conscience (later equity) clearer. Until 1957 the only legal penalty for murder was death. So in the law courts this was the only sentence ever passed; law courts exist to administer law. But the Home Secretary, acting as adviser to the monarch, dealt in a different commodity, *mercy*, and would, in appropriate cases, where the individual circumstances of the case seemed to require it, recommend the grant of a remission of the death penalty in the exercise of the prerogative of mercy. Thus one set of institutions, the courts, dealt in law, whilst another institution, the Home Office, modified the rigours of the law by dealing in mercy. No contradiction is involved, for obviously the law can be enforced with or without mercy. Similarly, legal rights can be exercised in conformity with good conscience, or not.

In the sixteenth century a different theory, which had had some following earlier, began to gain ground; it was that the Chancellors were administering not conscience, but *equity*. The idea was derived from the writings of Aristotle. He had argued in the *Nichomachean Ethics* that law, which operates through general rules in the pursuit of justice, is inevitably imperfect, because it is impossible ever to formulate a general rule which will satisfactorily cope with all the circumstances which will arise. Human beings just cannot anticipate the infinite complexities of the future, and hence cannot provide for them. So if justice is to be done we need not just rules, but a power to depart from them when they produce unjust results. It is the generality of rules which is the trouble, but it is the generality of a prescription that makes it a rule. An example may make the problem clear. Suppose we have a rule that the children are always to have a bath before going to bed, which seems a sensible enough rule. Obviously there need to be exceptions. For example, it would be silly to insist on a bath if one of the children was critically ill with pneumonia. We could try to think of all the exceptions in advance, but the task is hopeless, as becomes clear on the day when, through an accident to a travelling circus, we find a spitting cobra in the bath. Nobody would ever have thought of that possibility, and provided for it by the spitting cobra exception. So we need a power, not itself governed by any rule, to depart from the rule, and this power was called equity. Another way of putting Aristotle's theory is to say that law is inherently imperfect. And so we need, in addition to law, a corrective to law.

In the early seventeenth century a classic statement of the theory of the Court of Chancery used both the older conception of conscience and the more modern theory of equity: 'The Office of the Chancellor is to correct men's consciences for frauds, breaches of trusts, wrongs and oppressions of whatever nature they be, *and to soften and modify the extremity of the law*.' It will be seen that the first part of this quotation deals with conscience, the second, which I have italicised, with equity.

In the course of time, although the two ideas survived, the name given to the theory of the court came to be equity, and by degrees the practices of the court came to be governed by more or less settled rules, just like the rules followed in the common law courts. Equity largely but not entirely came to abandon its discretionary character, and could be as rigid as law itself. Indeed it became no more than another body of law, enforced in a distinct court. The same thing happened in relation to the prerogative of mercy: rules were developed as to when the sentence of death would not be carried out, and precedents established. But an element of real discretion remained.

It was possible to present the activities of the Court of

Chancery as involving a conflict with the common law. In our example of the trust this would mean that the common law said the trustees owned the property, the Chancellor said the infant son was the owner. If the relationship was viewed in terms of a conflict, it came to be settled, after some controversy, that equity prevailed over law, and this rule is now statutory. But the orthodox theory of the matter is that no conflict is involved. Equity presupposes the existence of law, and merely insists, where the particular circumstances of the case require this, that the application of the law shall be modified so as to achieve the end of law, which is justice. So it is the function of equity to fulfil the law, not undermine it. In our example the Chancellor, according to this way of talking about the matter, does not in any way dispute the fact that the two friends are legal owners of the property. He merely insists that they should not make use of their ownership in a way which violates the trust placed in them.

The institutional distinction between law and equity was abolished in England in 1876; all courts now adminster law and equity. But in the common law world the rules developed in the common law courts are still to a considerable degree thought of as a separate entity from those evolved in the Court of Chancery. Thus the common law's remedy for a broken contract, damages, is governed by quite different rules from equity's remedy, an order that the contract be performed (known as a decree of specific performance). The latter is still to some degree a discretionary remedy, which a court can refuse if it seems innappropriate in the circumstances. So the conceptual distinction between the two systems lives on, as does the somewhat strange idea that all the conclusions of equity stem from a very small number of principles of justice – the so called 'maxims of equity' – which have a certain comical character – 'he who comes to equity must have clean hands', 'equity is equality', 'equity does nothing in vain', 'equity regards the substance and not the form.'

SOME PROBLEMS OF NOMENCLATURE

We may conclude this chapter by mentioning some confusions of nomenclature. The basic meaning of the common law is that it is the law available to everyone in the realm; it is not local, or personal to certain groups only. The expression comes by degrees to be firmly associated with the royal courts which developed the law which was common in this sense. Until the structure of the courts was altered in 1876 these were the courts of King's Bench, Common Pleas and Exchequer, which all sat in the law terms in Westminster Hall in London, a building which of course still exists. These were called the Courts of Common Law. Since the law was the law of these courts, and developed by the judges in them, common law comes to carry the sense of judge-made law, as opposed to law laid down in statutory form by Parliament. So the term is often used in a way which contrasts common law with statute law. What went on in the Chancellor's Court was not law at all, but conscience or equity; hence sometimes the term common law is used in opposition to equity. But this is not always the case, for sometimes the term common law is applied more generally to the whole system of law evolved in England, and extended in the course of time to Wales, Ireland and, through British sea power and enterprise, to the overseas territories of the Empire and Colonies. So we speak of the common law system or tradition as including equity and such things as the assumptions which go to make up the system of parliamentary constitutionalism. Finally, as we have seen, Roman law can be called the common law of Europe, just to be awkward; confusion is here often avoided by using the Latin term, *ius commune*. Purists may wish to muddy the waters further by pointing out that the traditional name for English law is *Lex et Consuetudines Anglie*, the law and customs of England, not common law at all. It all sounds terribly confusing, but the context usually makes matters clear.

4

The Divisions of the Law

Just as history is divided up into subjects, such as economic history, political history, military history, European history and modern history, so too is the law. In a system which has grown up in a piecemeal and disorderly way, as has the common law, working out a method of classifying the law has presented serious difficulties. It was only in the seventeenth century that any satisfactory general scheme was evolved by an unusually intelligent judge called Mathew Hale, though he himself did not live to make much use of it. But about a century later it was used by Sir William Blackstone as a basis for his *Commentaries on the Laws of England* – the first comprehensive and readable account of English law ever written, and, curiously enough, the last. Now as can be seen in the illustrations I have given of possible subdivisions of history, there can be very different ways of dividing up historical material – by reference to the aspect of human social life involved (economic history), by reference to period (modern history), by reference to the geographical area concerned (European history), and so forth. Then there can be classifications related to the attitude of the historian, such as 'Marxist' history, or 'Whig' history. In the same way classifications of the law and legal materials differ widely, depending upon the purpose for which they have been designed and the way in which they have been evolved.

One very down to earth purpose served by classifying legal materials, and indirectly the law, is that of making information easier to find, typically in a law library. Given only a small number of law books they can be conveniently arranged by size, by colour, by author or title alphabetically, or even by date of purchase; it will not much matter. Even if we keep them in a heap under the bed individual volumes will be quite easy to find. But a large collection, if it is to be easy to use, has to be divided up in a more sophisticated manner, according to the ways in which lawyers think about the law. So library classifications subdivide by *jurisdiction* (Scots law, French law, the law of England and Wales), by *source* of legal material (statutes, case reports, treatises) or by *subject matter* (contract law, property law, criminal law, planning law). Such library classifications are severely practical in function; they simply enable lawyers to find the books they need. But for lawyers, confronted with massive quantities of legal texts, this is a very important function. Hence one of the first jobs of a law student is to familiarise himself with such classifications so as to be able to find the books he needs. Indeed it is often said, with some justification, that a good lawyer does not need to know the law, but merely how and where to look it up.

Today the development of the computer has made possible electronic storage of much legal material, such as statutes, regulations and case reports, and in addition has made it possible to obtain access to such material in new ways. These cut across traditional legal categories, and can in fact be invented by the seeker after information to suit his particular problem. You can, for example, ask the machine to find all cases decided by the Court of Appeal containing the word 'bananas' in the unlikely event that this may prove useful (suppose you have a case involving a dispute over an import tax on bananas). Any word or group of words can be used, and they may be combined with established categories in order to narrow down the hunt. But this sort of possibility does not render the established categories obsolete, for law just depends upon systems of classification for its existence. And, useful though they are, computers with their hideous screens and irritating stupidity have no chance yet of supplanting the printed book as a storage mechanism for texts. For many purposes books have not been improved upon. So lawyers, for the foreseeable future, are going to continue to use the dusty tomes of the law as they have done for many centuries.

The divisions of the law, in terms of which lawyers think, are not simply arbitrary ways of sorting out a mass of legal materials into conveniently small heaps. They also reflect basic ideas about the structure or purpose of the law, for each category, be it what we think of as a discrete branch of the law, say criminal law or contract law, or some broader analytic division, such as public law or international law, is thought to possess a natural under-lying unity, which justifies its use as an organizing category. This unity will usually be found to lie either in the subject matter of the branch of law in question, that is to say the area of life with which it is concerned, or alternatively with its supposed general function.

Matters would be simpler if the divisions which are in use were all entirely rational and defensible, but in fact this is not the case, because here, as throughout the law, thought is much influenced by tradition. So ways in which the law was classified in the past tend to persist, even though they may not be ideal for the conditions of today. They resemble room divisions in an old historic house, one of the things those who like old buildings have to live with, even though housekeeping would be more rationally organized by enlarging the kitchen and making the scullery smaller. For everything in the law, like everything in literature, is affected by the past. An up-to-the-minute, state-of-the-art, legal system is something which, in the very nature of law, cannot ever exist. Even countries which have full-blooded revolutions find, if they are going to have law at all, that the pre-revolutionary system will largely persist. This happened, for example, in Russia after the Bolshevik Revolution of 1917. Again in Germany after Hitler came to power there was much official illegality by members of the party, who were in some ways above the law, and some dreadful laws of a racial type were passed, but most of the law went on much as before, and remains in force today in the new West German state; contract law is an example.

CLASSIFICATIONS BASED ON SUBJECT MATTER

Divisions of the law based on subject matter produce some of the more entertaining titles for legal books, for example R. C. Maxwell's *Law Relating to Slaughter Houses and Unsound Food*, which burst upon the legal world in 1925, or Messrs Polson, Brittain and Marshall's *The Disposal of the Dead* of 1953, a work not of embalming, or grave-digging, or cannibalism, but of law. When such classifications are based upon some everyday notion, such as that of a dog or dog owner (M. R. Emanuel's *The Law of Dogs* or W. M. Freeman's *Law of Dogs and Their Owners*), they are said to be *fact based*. If the organizing conception has been much refined and elaborated by lawyers, then the classification is said to be *legal*; it depends upon a concept elaborated by professional lawyers for their special purposes.

An example is the law of contract. This branch of the law deals with the legal effects of agreements in the civil law, that is in the branch of the law which is not concerned with criminal punishments. The law of contract deals with the principles and rules which are intended to tell you how a legally effective contract is made, and what remedies the law offers if such a contract has been broken. In short, contract law is about agreements and promises. Now we all have an everyday notion of what is meant by an agreement or a promise, and what it means to break one, and it might seem at first sight that the ideas involved are essentially simple. But the law of contract is far from simple. What counts as an agreement or a promise, for legal purposes, has been enormously elaborated by lawyers and courts. They have been playing around with these ideas for many centuries now, and have developed complex ideas on the matter not simply out of perversity, nor in response to imaginary problems and difficulties, but in response to real ones. In doing so they have come up with solutions of one kind and another which, tidied up and transmitted as a tradition, constitute the law of contract. In this process the lawyers' conception of what counts as a contract, or a breach of contract, and so forth, has long since parted company with the uninstructed common-sense notions of the layman about agreements and promises.

This process of elaboration and separation has come about for a variety of reasons. Sometimes questions of general social policy have been involved – the law has, for example, decided not to enforce many social arrangements, such as an arrangement to go on a picnic, even though an agreement is certainly involved. To exclude such arrangements there has evolved a legal doctrine which holds that only agreements *intended to have legal consequences* are in law enforceable contracts; this doctrine is supposed to enable a lawyer to tell which agreements are legally binding and which not. So the lay conception of an agreement, and the legal conception of a contract, have, in this instance, parted company. Sometimes the elaboration arises because the law has to be very precise in matters over which, in everyday life, precision is simply not needed. For example, suppose a contract is made by telephone, or telex, between England and France, and a dispute breaks out over it. What law is to apply, English law or French law? They may be different in some relevant way, so that the outcome of the case will turn on which system is applicable. A sensible rule might be to apply the law of the country where the contract was made. But to apply this the court must have some way of telling precisely where it was made, a matter which outside the law would not be of any interest or significance; indeed the question seems a very peculiar one. One way of answering it might be to analyse all contracts into an offer by one side and an acceptance by the other, and say that the contract is made where the acceptance took place, for it is at the moment of acceptance that the agreement is complete. Another possible way out of the difficulty would be to say that the applicable law should be the law governing the country where the contract was to be performed. There are other possible solutions, but the basic point is that the law has to give a precise answer to a real problem to which mere common sense provides no real guidance. It reacts to this need by becoming increasingly elaborate.

Sometimes the law's complexities reflect a desire both for precision and for equal treatment. Suppose, for example, we agree that contract breakers should, at least as a general rule, pay money compensation for breach of contract. This much seems fair, and in accordance with common sense. Obviously if the right to compensation is to be governed by law, and not simply depend upon the whims of the judge in each particular case, lawyers need to know as precisely as possible how to calculate the size of the bill. They need a rule or principle to guide them. But do we need just one principle, or should different principles govern different sorts of contracts, or different sorts of breaches, so that, for example, we have one rule for deliberate breaches, and another for accidental breaches? And what should the law aim to do in providing compensation? There are various possibilities. Shall we try to restore the two people to the situation they were in before the contract was made? Or to the position they would have been in if the contract had been performed? Or just require them to hand back anything they have received? If the law is to regulate the matter it will need to develop rules as precise as possible on such questions, and if it is to be just, it must treat all contract breakers the same, in so far as there exists no relevant difference between them. These difficulties arise in real life, not in imagination. Suppose, to take a practical example, a ship, part paid for, has been delivered late by the shipbuilder. Should the buyer be compensated for loss of the profits he says he would have made if the ship had arrived on time? Or should he just get enough money to hire a substitute ship for the interim period? Should he have a right to reject the ship and get his money back? If so, should he get interest on the money? And, whatever rules we adopt, should they apply to building contracts, or contracts of employment, as well?

Again, consider the question of excuses. Should contract law require the contractor to do his best, or require him to succeed or pay damages? And suppose that the situation when the contract was made is very different from the situation when it has to be performed: for example, there is a national rail strike in operation, or a war has broken out. Should this make a difference? Or suppose the contract was entered into under a serious mistake.

Over the course of the years the process of elaboration, a response to real problems arising in litigation, can produce a massive body of principles and rules and doctrines and distinctions, aimed at providing consistent guidance as to how such problems should be resolved. Now at one level the law of contracts will never become completely divorced from the lay conception of an agreement, and will continue to be based upon the simple idea that you should keep your promises, perform your agreements and satisfy the legitimate expectations to which agreements and promises give rise. Indeed at this level the whole of the law of contracts can be presented as a fairly simple statement, along these lines: *those who break binding contracts without a legitimate excuse must compensate the innocent party for the loss they cause, and may in appropriate cases be compelled to perform their contracts*. Indeed any branch of the law can be reduced to simple statements of this kind; the original French Civil Code covers what we call tort law in five articles containing, in all, just over 150 words. Thus one article, Article 1382, reads laconically: 'Tout fait quelconque de l'homme, qui cause à autrui un dommage, oblige celui par la faute duquel il est arrrivé, à le réparer.' You could hardly be simpler than that. But every term in this short statement of law has been enormously elaborated, as has every term in our statement of contract law. Indeed a book on the law of contract, or any other elaborated body of law, seems to be largely concerned with definition, with saying what, for legal purposes, a *legally binding contract* is, what *compensate* means, and so forth. Similarly books on criminal law present the law as being largely concerned with definitions, with defining concepts such as *murder*, or *malice aforethought*, or *theft*, or *robbery*

You might imagine that after, in some instances, centuries of work the lawyers would at last get a branch of the law, like contract law, into a state in which all uncertainties had been removed, and all problems solved, so that the lawyers could retire. But in fact this never happens, and there are a number of reasons for this. The first is that attitudes in society as to what the law of contract should be change; today, for example, there is more feeling in favour of protecting consumers against tough contracts than there was in the past. The second is the inherent imperfection of law which Aristotle pointed out so long ago, and which was thought to give rise to the need for equity, a discretionary modification of the law in the light of tricky cases which could not itself be reduced to rule. The third is that it is in the nature of those very general principles upon which the law is premised that they can suggest conflicting solutions in particular cases. This happens in everyday life; if we make it a principle not to cause distress to others and to tell the truth, what are we to do when Susan asks whether her new and hideous dress has been a good buy? The law is often like that, pulled in two directions. The fourth is that the law uses language, and language is imprecise. So all the solutions reached by courts can, through their imprecision, give rise to future borderline tricky cases.

There is another and perhaps more fundamental reason. Suppose we have a law in the form of a text: 'All those who bring cats into the college are to be expelled.' And suppose we leave the application of this law to the facts of cases to the Principal of the college, without expecting her to give any reasons at all for decisions to expel except this text. Under this system the law will simply be the proposition quoted. But once we start requiring her to give reasons, and require her to act consistently, the complexity of the law will increase; rulings as to what counts as a cat will become as important as the original text, and these rulings will then form a jumping off point for further arguments and rulings. So the boundary between law and fact will both move and expand, and after fifty years we shall have a huge body of learning about every word in the original law. It is therefore the pursuit of rationality and consistency that makes law endlessly more elaborate and complex. So long as courts adopt the practice of giving reasons for decisions, these reasons generate further argument in future cases. The process of legal elaboration can only be stopped by muzzling judges, as juries are muzzled; since juries give no reasons their decisions in tricky cases generate no law. Another way of putting this point is that whatever reasons juries have do not enter the known tradition, and therefore do not form part of the material whose re-interpretation is the constant business of the lawyers.

THE CORE SUBJECTS IN THE LEGAL CURRICULUM

The academic training of lawyers largely concentrates, especially at an early stage, upon branches of the law organized around artificial and abstract legal categories which have been highly elaborated. Examples, in addition to the law of contract, are the law of torts, of property in land, of trusts and of criminal law. Lawyers do not learn the business of the law by studying the law of mobile homes, of infectious diseases, or of muskrats, although there is law on all these subjects. There is a good reason for this. Branches of the law which have been highly elaborated provide the best vehicle for gaining understanding and expertise in the casuistic and analytical skills which expert lawyers sell to the public. It is in highly developed branches of the law that these skills have been most fully deployed, and it is therefore to these branches of the law that learners need to go to find models to emulate if they are to acquire the special skills of lawyers.

The reason why some areas of law become highly elaborated, and others not, does not necessarily reflect the intrinsic complexity of life in the area in question, but simply the amount of time and effort which expert lawyers have been prepared to invest in it. This has been determined principally by economic considerations. The problems of the poor are as complex and surely more pressing than those of the rich, but they do not feature so prominently in the law reports. Thus the law of property in land, which was where the money was, and to some extent still is, has been the subject of enormous investment of ingenuity over the centuries. The law of taxation is a modern example. Sometimes the elaboration is not simply explicable in so unglamorous a way. A student of criminal law will soon notice the almost incredible refinement of the distinction between the crime of murder and that of manslaughter. Until recently those who murdered might be hanged, whilst those who committed manslaughter ran no such risk, so this frontier was, surely rightly, treated as of critical importance. The law of parking without paying on the other hand is rudimentary in its simplicity. If the penalty were death it would not be. We should have long since developed concepts of transient immobility, excusable breakdown, the nature of intent to park, and so forth.

In the jargon of the trade it has come to be the practice to talk of the subjects on which law students cut their teeth as the *core* subjects; in addition to those which have been mentioned (contract, tort, property, trusts and criminal law) the canon currently includes constitutional and administrative law, this being one subject, not two. Tradition as well as rationality has had a hand in creating this list.

CONTRACT LAW

Contract law has already been mentioned and briefly described. Its claim to a central position in legal education has not been unchallenged in recent times, for some have argued that contract, like God, is probably dead. Its position in the scheme of things was established in the nineteenth century, at a time when there was a belief amongst intellectuals in social progress. Contract law was conceived to be an instrument through which this could be achieved. The argument, developed by Sir Henry Maine in his legal best seller, *Ancient Law*, was in outline this. In earlier forms of society, for example in feudal times, the position of the individual in society, his rights and duties and obligations, were largely determined by his fixed legal position, or status, in society. This was normally determined by his birth, though occasionally people might change their status, for example by becoming a monk, which brought about what was called civil death, or by marriage, or ennoblement. But in a society more flexibly regulated by the law of contract the rights, duties and obligations of an individual would be determined not by birth, but by the contracts which he freely chose to make. Hence the law of contract was thought to present a framework within which individuals could plan, organize and reorganize their own lives by mutual co-operation. Contract was therefore an instrument of freedom, and in so far as it places shackles upon us it only does so with our own consent. Of course what contracts a person could make would depend upon what contracts other people would be willing to make, as happens in a market, a place where people gather to buy and sell, and make other contracts. In such markets, by hosts of individual decisions, in which citizens pursue their own self-interest, exchange is organized and wealth both distributed and enhanced.

In a society organized by contract the whole society is likened to a market in which people are free to deal as they like with each other, certain forms of bad behaviour such as cheating being excluded. Ideas of this kind have long been popular with those who, in the tradition of Adam Smith, extol the virtues of the free market economy, an economy thus organized; the freedom in question today being not freedom from status, so much as freedom from central governmental control, or what is often called by those who approve of it, planning, and by those who do not, interference. Furthermore the free market economy is thought, of its very nature, to enhance human welfare. I exchange my apple for your banana because I want the banana more than I want the apple, and vice versa. As if by magic, we both end up better off. I am happier with my banana, and you with your apple, and even if we are not, we have nobody to blame but ourselves. Free marketeers usually claim that in general people are the best judge of their own self-interest. And so, the argument goes, in a world in which there is free exchange, we shall all be better off, and *we* decide what 'better' means.

Allied to notions of the value of the free market economy contract law became viewed as a branch of the law of pre-eminent social importance. So the working out in detail of the rules of law which gave precision to the idea of the freely negotiated agreement, and specified the extent to which it should be enforced, possessed an obvious intellectual interest. It so happened that in the nineteenth century the law of contract was much elaborated, and extensively influenced by ideas plagiarised from the civil law. So, in the late nineteenth century, the early days of university legal education, contract law assumed the centre of the stage, and has remained there ever since.

Today many people, especially those of left-wing views, are less confident in the absolute merits of the free market economy than once was the case. The trouble, some think, is that too much freedom here leads to unacceptable levels of inequality; the very successful contract makers become too rich. And so, it is argued, freedom produces inequality and inequality a lack of real freedom. There is less confidence too in the premise of freedom of choice which classical contract law assumed, and more consciousness too of the extent to which contractual arrangements affect people other than the immediate contracting parties. In consequence the law now seems to exhibit strong tensions, for example between the notion that it should uphold the sanctity of freely negotiated contracts, even if they seem one-sided, and the notion that the law should adopt a paternalistic stance and protect those who make bad bargains from what is often called exploitation. However these tensions are resolved the law of contract remains central to legal education and basic to social life as we know it, and its fascination has not been reduced by an increased uncertainty as to what it is all about, or even by the arguments of iconoclastic thinkers who have suggested that its more elaborate and intellectually interesting doctrines rarely if ever have much practical connection with the resolution of contractual disputes in real life.

THE LAW OF TORTS

The law of torts, or civil wrongs, seems at first sight something more of a rag bag, and perhaps it is. It consists of the law governing wrongs (such as trespass to land, false imprisonment, libel and slander, nuisance, and the negligent infliction of injury) which can be defined negatively in that they do not happen to consist either in the breach of agreements or in breaches of trusts. By a civil wrong is meant a wrong whose remedy is primarily intended to help the victim, for example, by compensating him in damages, and not to punish the wrongdoer. In fact many actions which amount to civil wrongs are also crimes: a thief can be both punished and made to pay compensation. But tort law is concerned only with the latter possibility. Whereas contractual obligations are usually voluntarily assumed, tort law duties are typically imposed upon us whether we like it or not.

This apparent unifying factor, together with the fact that tort law is mainly concerned with compensation for injury, has suggested to some writers that tort law ought in principle to be based upon a single theory of civil liability. But not everyone would agree with this. Some would argue that it is not at all obvious that the law of torts does exhibit any natural unity. The remedies which the law of torts provides seem to protect a variety of different interests, such as the interest in physical safety, in reputation, in personal freedom, in privacy, and so forth. Given this diversity of function it is questionable whether the same theory of liability should cover all these interests alike. For example, the law might be stricter in its protection of personal freedom than in protecting personal reputation.

As the matter currently stands the law of torts appears to reflect a tension between two different theories of civil liability. According to one, liability should exist either when there is deliberately inflicted injury, or fault in the rather artificial sense of a failure to exhibit the standard of care which might be expected of a reasonable person, the reasonable man or woman of the common law. According to the alternative theory liability should not depend on fault at all. It should be strict, and lie on the person whose activities have caused or enabled the loss to occur. Other versions of this second theory would place the loss on the person profiting from the activity, or on the person who is in the best position to prevent such losses occurring. Theories of this type start from the fact that if loss occurs, someone is going to have the pay the bill, and unless the victim caused the loss the obvious person is the person who caused the loss to occur. The fascination in studying tort law lies both in the fundamental nature of the questions at issue – when should one person compensate another for loss caused by his activities? – and by the extraordinary wealth and variety of the incidents which have over the years given rise to litigation in the courts. It is a subject which law students never find boring, though they do often find it disorderly and confusing.

THE LAW OF PROPERTY

Property law is one of the more weird subjects at the centre of the legal curriculum. As we have seen, the allocation of wealth and its protection has always been a central function of law, and in consequence the law of property was the branch of the law which first became highly elaborated. Those who possessed wealth were naturally prepared to employ it to protect their assets in litigation, and property, it must be remembered, is closely associated with power and status and social obligation, as well as with mere subsistence. Owning a Porsche or Rolls-Royce is not just owning a way of getting about; you can do that in comfort for a fraction of the price. Again much of the vast acquisition and transfer of property at Christmas is a response to the obligation to give gifts, and to accept them, whether we like it or not, and however useless they may be as simple utilitarian objects. So property has a variety of meanings, and always has had. Long before the close of the medieval period the law of property had become very complicated indeed. This however came about at a time when the principal form of wealth was land and assets closely associated with land, such as castles, and fishing rights, and rights to pasture animals on other people's land. We can lump all these assets together and call them forms of immovable property. The technical term used by lawyers came to be *real* property. From the beginnings of the common law until the nineteenth century it was the law of real property which attracted most legal ingenuity. Landed wealth was particularly important as the economic basis of the family life of the upper classes, and alliances between powerful families, forged through marriage, which had nothing to do with falling in love, were accompanied by complex marriage gifts, called settlements, designed to organize the enjoyment of wealth and the perpetuation of family power. The law governing other forms of property was not so highly developed in earlier times. In the medieval period even the rich owned little in the way of movable property, though certain forms of such property, for example cattle, horses, armour and mass books, were the subject of considerable investment. Much spare wealth went to the church, for example in reliquaries to hold the relics of saints, sometimes even mixed saints (*sancti mixti*) when pieces had become muddled up.

The consequence was that the highly developed law was land law. It concerned those forms of wealth which were most amply protected by being made specifically recoverable by an action in the courts. One of the characteristics of land is that it rarely goes away, except on riversides and the sea coast, and cannot be hidden, so that it is practicable to protect rights in it this way. Land, in a sense, just cannot be stolen. The law governing other forms of property, movable property, or as lawyers call it, personal property, was relatively undeveloped, and treated merely as an aspect of the tort actions which could be used to remedy such wrongs as detaining other people's goods. The main protection for personal property was, in any event, the criminal law, not the civil law at all; thieves of any consequence could be hanged, and the lives of lesser thieves made suitably miserable. Thieves are no longer hanged, but to this day the main protection offered by the law to owners of personal property is the criminal law, and the law of contract, under which such property is often insured against loss through theft. In theory you can sue thieves for damages but hardly anybody ever does. Getting money out of serious thieves is all but impossible.

By the close of the fifteenth century there had been written a celebrated textbook on the law of real property; the author was a judge, one Thomas Littleton, and you can see his tomb to this day in the cathedral at Worcester. He was a remote ancestor of the jazz musician Humphrey. His real memorial is however not

British jazz but his book, *Littelton's Tenures*, and for three-and-a-half centuries the lot of the law student was to study this work, encased in an elaborate commentary by Sir Edward Coke, hence *Coke on Littleton*, as an essential preliminary to learning the law of property. It was not a happy lot, for *Coke on Littleton*, which embodies in its final form Hargrave's notes, to Butler's notes, to Hale's notes, to Coke's notes to Littleton, is a repulsive work. The modern law student is spared this penance, but reads its successors, none of which are light reading, for to this day the law of property as studied in law courses largely means the law of property in immovables. This law is expressed in a strange late medieval terminology. Lawyers when they are being purists do not talk about an *owner* of a house, but of a *tenant in fee simple absolute in possession*; they employ a language developed centuries ago in the time of the Wars of the Roses to express the complicated landholding arrangements of that earlier world. Many of the terms used are of Norman French derivation, for this was the language of the landed aristocracy and one which survived into the seventeenth century as a private written language used only by the lawyers who served their interests.

The law of landed property was brought to its highest state of complexity when employed in the property settlements, designed as we have seen to underpin the dynastic family arrangements of the wealthy, particularly alliances through marriage. Strange legal doctrines, such as the rule against perpetuities, much celebrated by lawyers for its air of deep mystery, were developed to prevent family property being too rigidly settled for all time by a landowner who imagined he could foresee the future. The study of this celebrated rule is still used to tease the brains of law students, and is agreed to be one of the most immediately incomprehensible branches of the common law. There is some doubt as to whether the rule serves any useful purpose at all today, and in some parts of the common law world it has been abolished completely without, so far, any obvious disasters or public campaigns to Bring Back the Rule Against Perpetuities. Who knows, they may come yet! So the law of property in land, as studied today, bears many marks of its earlier history, and its esoteric character fascinates some law students whilst, it must be admitted, repelling others. It largely consists of those parts of the law which must be known for the practise of conveyancing, that is the creation and transfer of rights of property in land, and conveyancing has now for over a century been a very profitable activity, largely dominated by solicitors. The law governing movable property remains curiously little studied in law courses, and branches of the law dealing with more modern forms of wealth, such as copyright, or shares in companies, have not yet displaced the gothic law of real property as the vehicle through which law students are introduced to the higher flights of legal imagination and something of the theatre of the absurd.

The law of trusts is really a subdivision of the law of property, and has its origin in the institutional division between the common law, administered in the courts of common law, and equity, administered in the Court of Chancery. At its simplest, as we have seen, a trust arises when property is given to someone, a trustee, or a number of trustees, on the understanding that the trustee (or trustees) is to hold and manage the property for the benefit of someone else, a beneficiary. A modern example would be the transfer of some stocks and shares to two local worthies on the understanding that the income from the property was to be used for the benefit of the village cricket club. The essential element here is the splitting apart of the right of management and control, which is given to the trustees, from the right of beneficial enjoyment, given to the beneficiary, the club. Usually these rights reside in a single owner; if I own an apple I can both sell it or give it away (management), or eat it (enjoyment). In a trust these aspects of ownership are split apart. The common law courts did not develop any scheme for protecting the intended beneficiary under trusts; he had, as we have seen, to turn to the Court of Chancery for protection. In time the Chancery developed elaborate traditional rules under which whilst the trustee, as owner in the eyes of the law, had the management powers, the beneficiary, viewed by equity as owner, had the right to enjoyment of the economic benefits of ownership.

Originating in a world which no longer exists, in which legal rights were enforced in one court and equitable in another, the institution of the trust has survived. Indeed it flourishes in modern society, in part because of the convenience of separating management and enjoyment, in part because of its flexibility in setting up family arrangements for the relatively affluent, and in part because of its utility in minimizing the incidence of unwelcome taxation. Like other more complex branches of the law of property, trust law departs from the simple model of one owner owning, by himself and for himself, one single thing. Company law, with directors and shareholders and employees, is an even more complex example. In modern times the property held under trust will rarely be a single specific object; more usually what is held in trust is a fund, a collection of assets (say a mixed bag of stocks and shares and a house) which may change in composition under the control of the trustees. Very large parts of the wealth of the country are held in this way, typically by the vast pension funds into which those of working age, and their employers, tuck away wealth to be drawn on in retirement. Such funds may include, in addition to more obvious assets, such things as paintings by Renoir and Georgian coffee pots, not to mention race horses or islands in the sun. Unit trusts are another example; investors buy shares in a trust fund, which is itself formed out of a large number of different stocks and shares, sometimes of a particular type, perhaps 'Far Eastern' or 'European'. The fund is managed by professionals on the investor's behalf. Participation in a mixed bag of shares has the attraction of reducing the risk of putting all your eggs in one basket, and many private investors have neither the skill nor inclination to manage their own savings.

PUBLIC AND PRIVATE LAW

Two of the core subjects which have not yet been described, constitutional and administrative law, and criminal law, illustrate another basic scheme for dividing up the law; according to this all law is either public law or private law. The former is concerned with the relationship between the individual or groups and the state, whereas the latter is concerned with the relationship between individuals or groups and each other. The subjects which we have so far mentioned all belong to private law; the two core subjects with which we are now concerned belong to public law. The distinction seems at first sight a simple and obvious one, but is not entirely free from difficulty for a variety of reasons. For example, many of the rules of private law apply to relations between the state and the individual as well, for the state, for some purposes, is treated just the same as a private individual. Again the theoretical position in the case of criminal prosecutions is that they all are taken on behalf of the Crown, so that all crimes are crimes against the state. So criminal law belongs to public law. But the reality of the matter is that many criminal prosecutions, for example prosecutions instigated by private individuals for assault, or by stores for shop-lifting, are ways of mediating quarrels between individuals. So the distinction between public and private law, though useful in its way, is a theoretical distinction which can, if taken too seriously, be rather misleading. Increased state intervention in what was once private has also tended to collapse the distinction.

Constitutional law is primarily concerned to investigate and expound the degree to which the ideal of the rule of law, that is the ideal of government through law, is reflected in the existing legal arrangements through which government is carried on. Hence it is concerned first of all with power, in particular with the legal rules according to which governmental powers are distributed between the legislature, the executive and the judiciary. Its subject matter here is the legal structures and institutions through which government operates. One important aspect of this distribution of power will be the limits which the law places upon governmental powers of one kind or another. So constitutional law is also much concerned with the accountability, or lack of it, of power holders, such as ministers, civil servants and others, for example intelligence services. One such limit can be the recognition of individual legal rights which constrain the exercise of governmental power in the name of some superior value, such as personal liberty, which is thought as it were to trump the claims of the state against its citizens. So a course on constitutional law will be much concerned with the questions of individual rights and the mechanisms, such as *habeas corpus*, whereby they are secured, if indeed they are secured. Another important aspect of the distribution of power is the position of the principal coercive organizations employed by the state when, to put it crudely but realistically, the boot is put in. They are the armed services, the police service and the prison service, potential friends of the rule of law, but potential enemies too. So constitutional lawyers are much concerned with the control over these services, and with the remedies which can be used if power is abused, though they often seem to forget the third member of this trinity.

The idea of a system of government wholly controlled by rules laid down in advance is an absurd one; for there to be government there must be areas of choice and discretion. Parliament must, for example, be free to choose between competing legislative policies and means of carrying them out; there would be little point in Parliaments and elections if everything was settled in advance by the law, which, like that of the Medes and Persians, altered not. So constitutional law is much concerned with discretionary power and the problem of keeping it within prescribed limits, and ensuring that it is not exercised upon improper grounds. Administrative law, which is a branch of constitutional law, deals in detail with the mechanisms whereby the courts exercise supervision over the organs of government in our much governed society.

Most countries in the world now possess a written constitution, and this forms a body of basic law, setting out, at least in outline, the structure of governmental organizations and their powers. Modern constitutions also specify basic constitutional rights and establish whatever system of internal checks and balances are thought appropriate to maintain the constitutional structure. Commonly they entrench certain provisions, that is to say make them difficult, or even impossible, to alter by legal methods. The most celebrated constitution is that of the United States of America, which, as it has come to be interpreted, gives the courts, and particularly the Supreme Court, very extensive powers of control over the federal and state legislatures. In particular the courts can refuse to apply laws, passed by Congress or state legislatures, which infringe provisions of the constitution. It was based upon the idea that citizens need protection from government even in a democracy. Britain does not possess a constitution in this sense, and in consequence the precise scope of what counts as constitutional law is somewhat uncertain. Even where such a constitution does exist, it will never in fact contain the whole of the law which governs the process of government, for much of this law resides not in the words of a text, but in the traditions within the legal community as to the appropriate place of law in government. Any study of constitutional law which is worth the candle will involve a study of these constitutional traditions and assumptions, as well as a study of the more formal legal materials. Constitutional law, and constitutional theory, are not usefully separated.

If the lack of a written constitution tends to make the scope of constitutional law rather uncertain, the secrecy which surrounds the processes of government in Britain may have the more serious consequence of rendering all accounts of British government, to a greater or less degree, mythical. It has long been recognized that the regulation of the processes of government in Britain has not been confined to regulation by rules enforceable in the courts. The Victorian constitutional guru Albert Venn Dicey gave the name 'conventions' to practises followed in government, but not enforceable by courts, for example the long-established convention that the monarch automatically gives consent to legislation passed by the House of Commons and House of Lords. In Britain government is very largely conducted by the professional civil service under some degree of control from Ministers and, very indirectly, from Parliament; no better account of this system exists than that provided in the television series *Yes Minister*. The practices and conventions followed within the largely hidden world of Whitehall are as important to the conduct of government as rules enforced in courts; unhappily knowledge of what they are is largely concealed. An intelligent study of constitutional government in Britain has to recognize this feature and avoid confusing the rhetoric of constitutional law, which tends to be the rhetoric of the rule of law, with reality.

CRIMINAL LAW

Criminal law is the branch of the law which most excites public interest and fascination. It lays down the circumstances in which citizens render themselves liable to suffer punishment at the hands of the state. This concern with punishment differentiates criminal law from civil law, which, at least as a general rule, is not in the business of punishing people. The central provisions of criminal law deal with forms of anti-social behaviour, such as murder and robbery and blackmail, which seem to be wholly incompatible with the preservation of orderly social life. In the past the graver crimes, those that is which were most feared, were called felonies, and rendered the offender liable to the punishment of death. So the essential function of basic criminal law was that of identifying people who needed to be eliminated from society in the most effective way, by killing them. In the course of time other forms of elimination were invented, first of all transportation, which survived into the 1860s, and then, as this became unnacceptable to the host countries, imprisonment, which has come to be the typical punishment of the criminal law of today. Even today people often talk of the imprisoned as if they did not exist, as if they actually had been eliminated. For example, it is often said that whatever its demerits imprisonment does at least prevent criminals committing crimes when they are inside, a view which only seems plausible if we think of prisons as being outside society. Of course lots of crimes are committed in prisons. With the rise of imprisonment, a phenomenon of the nineteenth century, the strange idea developed that people might even be improved and made into better persons by being imprisoned, a notion which lingers on today, though I doubt if anyone who knows much about prisons takes it very seriously. But the punishments of traditional criminal law have never been primarily directed to making silk purses out of sows' ears. Their function, in addition to elimination, has been partly that of terrorising others into conformity with society's demands (today called deterrence), and partly that of giving the criminal his just deserts, so as to restore a sort of equilibrium in society between good and evil. Elimination and deterrence are practical aims, retribution a moral aim; it is quite impossible to grasp the significance of criminal law without realizing that it has a moral purpose as well as a purely practical one.

Even traditional criminal law in its harshest days never carried out all its threats; the definitions of crimes swept into the net all sorts of people who, though technically murderers, or robbers, or whatever, excited some sympathy, and who were treated more leniently than strict law suggested they would be, for example by being pardoned by the Crown. The system always engaged in a form of overkill, and this remains true to this day, with the consequence that many fairly harmless people, whose activities constitute a minor nuisance at worst, count as criminals. So there have developed a host of lesser forms of punishment, or 'treatment', which can be employed to avoid the imposition of sentences of imprisonment upon such persons. Examples are probation orders, and compulsory 'community service'. Often these treatments are claimed to make people better, to reform them. Perhaps they occasionally do, but in the main they are simply excuses for not doing something nastier.

On to the stock of traditional basic criminal law has been grafted a whole apparatus of coercive governmental control which is a by product of the increased scale of government over the last century or so. State agencies of one kind or another have taken to regulating an incredible range of activities – the hours shops can remain open, when drinks can be bought, where dogs may defecate, the conditions under which one can pierce ears for gain, or practice acupuncture, who can offer conveyancing for reward, or hold themselves out as medically qualified, what trees may be cut down, what sorts of seed may be sold. The job of giving teeth to all this regulatory activity has been handed over to the same courts who have traditionally dealt with crime. The usual punishment associated with what have come to be called regulatory offences is the fine, though in many cases there is a possibility of imprisonment to deal with the wholly non-co-operative. So criminal law, once concerned merely to protect individuals from the grosser forms of anti-social behaviour, has come to be used as the instrument of modern regulatory government. It is used to deal with those whose 'crime' consists in not doing as they are told.

Courses for law students in the criminal law tend to concentrate attention upon traditional real crimes, such as murder and manslaughter and theft, and although this somewhat distorts the picture of the criminal law it is understandable enough. For it is the traditional criminal law which represents the most extreme interference by the state in the lives of its citizens: to be imprisoned, even for a short period, is to be completely expelled from normal social life. So traditional criminal law raises basic questions of the ethics of punishment and coercion; it is an area in which moral questions and legal questions merge into each other. One such question centres upon the notion of personal responsibility for our actions. Traditional criminal law is based upon the idea that as a general rule (if we exclude the insane, the very young and the physically coerced) human beings are responsible for what they choose to do, and if they choose to commit crimes to the harm of others it is they who really send themselves to prison. They deserve punishment by choosing the evil path. In everyday life we often act on this assumption, and yet we also and somewhat inconsistently think that what people do is often conditioned by their circumstances of life, so that they do not really have a free choice. Often this sort of claim is presented in a court as being relevant to the sentence: the unhappy child of the bad home could not fully help himself, and his burning down of the local comprehensive was, as the social workers say, 'a cry for help'. In the criminal law the conflict between theories of personal responsibility and theories of social conditioning by circumstances are endlessly played out. An example in modern case law involves the question whether it should be a defence to a charge of murder that the killer would have been in danger of death himself if he had not killed an innocent third party. Is such a person really deserving of severe punishment? Is he really responsible for his action? So criminal law tends to fascinate students with a philosophical turn of mind. It also, through its connection with punishment, tends to polarise individuals into hawks and doves.

It is also a branch of the law replete with fine distinctions, distinctions upon which may turn the difference between going to prison and leaving court without a stain on your character. The case law is full of instances, such as this. A greyhound fancier and punter places a bet on a particular animal; this stake is returnable if the stewards for any reason declare 'No race' to have taken place. But if the chosen dog simply fails to win, the stake is of course lost. Observing his chosen hound to be tardy and unenthusiastic in leaving the traps, and thus unlikely to win, the accused leapt on to the track, hoping thereby to disrupt the proceedings and induce the stewards to declare 'No race' so that his stake will not be lost to him. The plan fails, as the race is not sufficiently disrupted for the stewards to act. Theft is legally defined as 'dishonestly appropriating property belonging to another . . .'; can the punter be convicted of *attempting* to steal the stake? Or take another modern case. A car driver, when parking, quite accidentally drives his car on to a policeman's foot. The policeman asks him to move the car off his foot. The driver, no lover of the constabulary, declines to do so and having applied the handbrake walks off. Has he assaulted the officer? How can you assault someone by doing nothing? Or did he do something? The person involved in this case was, believe it or not, called Fagan.

INTERNATIONAL LAW AND MUNICIPAL LAW

One value commonly associated with law is, as we have seen, order; indeed many think that in the absence of law, social order is impossible of achievement. The worst forms of disorder to which human societies are prone, if we exclude natural catastrophes such as famine or earthquake, or epidemic disease, are experienced in times of revolution (when a legal order is in a state of collapse) or in times of war, when conflicts between states degenerate into partially organized violence. Since law, by providing mechanisms for the peaceful resolution of conflicts and rules for mutual forbearance and co-operation, can produce order within a society, it seems at least in principle possible that it can perform the same role in ordering relationships between states. The belief in this ideal has given rise to what is known as public international law, so called to differentiate it from a subject called either private international law or conflict of laws. The latter deals with the recognition by one legal system of the rules of another legal system. For example, suppose a couple who have been married in Russia according to Russian law have emigrated to France and adopted children there. They then make a will and die on holiday in a road accident in Spain. Their legal position obviously presents tricky problems if litigation arises in England between their adopted children over their holiday home here. What law is to govern the matters in dispute? Private international law grapples with these problems. Public international law on the other hand is concerned not directly with the legal position of individuals, but with the legal relationships between states.

The founder of modern international law was a seventeenth-century Dutch scholar, Hugo Grotius, and his classic work on the subject is called *De Iure Belli et Pacis, Concerning the Law of War and Peace*. The title seems at first sight odd, for how can there can be a law of war, when war is the very antithesis of law? But one admittedly modest step towards a more ordered relationship between states was to attempt to regulate the violence of war, in

108

much the same way as the violence of boxing was regulated by the Queensberry Rules so as to reduce, albeit marginally, its brutality in the bare knuckle days. But this did not involve an attempt to abolish boxing. Similarly in the law of pre-conquest England it was idle to attempt to abolish the blood feud, but the law did attempt to regulate it and provide, in the payment of money composition, an alternative to it; and although such feuds can still go on, in general they do not, the first step to their abolition being modest in scope. Attempts to minimize the suffering caused by war have had some limited successes, at least in Europe. An example is the outlawing of gas warfare, and another is the amelioration in the lot of prisoners of war under the Geneva Conventions.

Merely to regulate war is hardly an exciting or optimistic end to seek through the introduction of law into the relationships between states. So international lawyers have attempted to build up a body of rules and doctrines whose more ambitious aim is peace. One way in which this can be achieved is through treaties and conventions between states, in effect contracts, and one of the basic principles of international law is embodied in the old legal maxim *pacta sunt servanda*, agreements are to be kept. So international law has a lot to say about treaties and other forms of international agreement. It also seeks to differentiate between justified and unjustified claims (for example, to territory or to offshore mineral rights), and, what is fundamental to law, distinguish between the legitimate and illegitimate use of violence. There has also been established in the United Nations a forum both for international co-operation and for ritualising international conflict into the exchange of formalised abuse, reminiscent of the Esquimaux song duels. Cynics may say that the whole institution is little more than an expensive talking shop, whilst others may feel that jaw-jaw is better than war-war.

International law, whatever its achievements, necessarily differs from municipal law in ordered societies in two critical respects. The first is that it lacks the institution of a court with compulsory jurisdiction; the so-called Court of International Justice is in fact a Board of Arbitration, whose power has to be voluntarily submitted to by the parties to a dispute. So international conflicts, if they are to be resolved peaceably, and very many are, have to be resolved by negotiation, mediation, or arbitration. The second is that the community of nations has not been able to develop a regular system of applying coercive force to the recalcitrant. A third weakness lies in the scale and diversity of the world in which international law is developed and used, which makes it extremely difficult to secure a general measure of agreement as to how the principles of international law apply to particular conflicts, such as, for example, Britain's conflict with Argentina over the Falkland/Malvinas Islands. International lawyers seek to find a basis for their views as to the rights and wrongs of disputes in treaties, in the practices followed by states and in the consensus of opinion amongst international legal scholars, and have had some success in their enterprise. Some would argue that international law's function is not so much that of imposing order on the community of nations, an impossible agenda in the absence of some overarching control by a superpower, but rather of providing a language and scheme of conceptions into which conflicts can be reduced and made subject of negotiation.

5

The Sources of Law

We have seen how in the common law system the typical form of law is case law, evolved over the course of time by the courts in deciding individual disputes brought before them in litigation. For many centuries legislation, that is to say deliberate avowed law making, expressed in the promulgation of authoritative texts, played a very small part indeed in the growth of the law. Law was normally something that existed as part of the natural fabric of the world, not something that was made. If its claim to be respected came into question there could be no appeal to the authority of a lawgiver, for there was no lawgiver, but only an appeal to its conformity with tradition, so that it expressed how things had always been, or to its intrinsic good sense. Such legislation as there was, affecting either private or public law, was exceptional, passed by Parliament more in the spirit of correcting some incidental defect in the working of the law being applied by the regular judges, rather than in any spirit of legal innovation. So orally transmitted court tradition, partially recorded in manuscript case reports, was the typical source of law, not the texts of statutes. But from the very earliest times although legislation was exceptional it did happen. Indeed the earliest document in the English language to have survived, though in a much later copy, consists of the laws of King Ethelbert of Kent, promulgated early in the seventh century. At this time judgements of the Royal Council would not have been clearly distinguished from general legislation by the same body, and the impetus behind the laws or dooms of Ethelbert may have come from St Augustine's mission, which threw up problems which could only be dealt with by a form of law making.

In the medieval period, although legislation remained relatively unusual, there were many statutes passed, particularly under Edward I, some of which had highly important effects on private law. For example, the Statute *De Donis Conditionalibus* ('Concerning Conditional Gifts'), which dates from 1285, became the source of the law governing entails of landed estates. But these early statutes became so overlaid by judicial interpretation as to be effectively incorporated into the common law. There was another flurry of legislative activity in Henry VIII's reign, associated with the breach with Rome, and more during the interregnum in the seventeenth century. This was succeeded by a period of legislative quiescence during the eighteenth and early nineteenth centuries, which ended with the Reform Act of 1832.

Over the many centuries during which legislation was relatively infrequent the common law, left to its own devices, evolved and expanded continuously. But the lawyers' theory of the matter, which originally was probably literally believed, denied this; it was that the common law had existed from time immemorial, and was a comprehensive and unchanging body of law, to be applied, not tinkered about with, by the judges. There probably still are a few common lawyers who believe something not far from this in a fairly literal sense, though it seems more sensible to view the theory as a sort of myth, which serves to present the practice of judicial decision as being in perfect conformity with the rule of law. Be that as it may, to this day considerable branches of the law owe little or nothing to legislation and, more importantly, the general structure of legal thought in the common law world is almost entirely a product of professional development in the courts.

LEGISLATION AND ITS INTERPRETATION

The relative importance of case law and statute has however changed. The rise in the scale of government in the nineteenth century, and the evolution of a centralised bureaucracy of professional experts in government, was accompanied by a huge increase in the scale of parliamentary legislation. The fact that at the beginning of the nineteenth century the Home Office occupied only two rooms may bring home the extent of the change. The two World Wars of this century, together with the increased influence of socialism on government, whatever the party in power, has continued the trend towards more govern-ment, and a principal instrument of government has been statute law. So today most law has as its point of departure an Act of Parliament; even those branches of the law which are basically of judicial origin, such as the law of contract or the criminal law, or the law of property in land, have everywhere been extensively modified by statute.

In the nineteenth century there also grew up a school of thought which favoured the codification of the common law, so that it too would be reduced to statutory form. The practice of codification had been adopted by some civil law countries, the most celebrated code being the French Civil Code, introduced in the belief that so long as the law was accurately and compre-hensively set out in a code, both the job of judges would be made simpler and citizens would know what the law was. Codification, besides being a move towards clarity and simplicity in the law, was also thought desirable as a way of reducing the status of judges, who would no longer be able to make law. Law would be made by the legislature, and through democratic procedures brought under popular control. In England the prime candidates for codification were criminal law and contract law, but the movement never succeeded at home, though codes became normal in colonial territories, which usually had a criminal code and a contract code. In America the codification movement took a curious form: academic lawyers produced codes called 'restatements' of the common law, and although they have no legislative backing they have become an important part of professional tradition. The failure to date of the codification movement in England did not however prevent the rise of much legislation modifying the common law.

So today statute law is everywhere of great importance in the practice of the law. Now it might be thought that the shift from cases to statutes, with their specific and authoritative texts, would both reduce the significance of judge-made law and increase the clarity and certainty of the law. This has not however proved to be the case. However carefully and meticulously a statute is drafted, and many are not, situations in which the application of the provisions of a statute to a particular case gives rise to controversy and doubt seem to be quite inevitable. Various legislators have believed that their laws will need no interpretation; Justinian thought this and so did lawyers in the early days of the Code Napoléon. They have always been wrong. There are three reasons for this.

The first is that statutes operate through the use of a natural language. Now the conceptions which are expressed in our language, and whose sharing enables us to communicate with each other, are inherently imprecise. In everyday communication this imprecision may not cause any problems, for expressions often derive clarity and precision from the context in which they are used. So, if we are in a room in which there is a stuffed cat, a china cat, a cat-o'-nine-tails and a female cat with five newly born kittens and you say 'Please feed the cat' I will know exactly what you mean; the mother cat will get the food. The context will make it all quite clear, and this context may include the fact that you are stroking the animal at the time when you speak. If of course the china cat was an idol and the available food had been blessed by the priests it might be clear that the food was for the idol.

Now consider the use of the conception of a cat, used, let us suppose, in the Cats Act 1984. The context in which this Act was passed might be a media-generated rabies scare, a much less precise context than exists in the face-to-face use of language for communication. Let us suppose that the Act, by section one, provides that it shall be a capital offence 'To bring, or cause to be brought into the United Kingdom, from any foreign port, any cat, without having obtained in advance a cat importer's certificate in accordance with the provisions of schedule 2 of this Act'. Snooks, a taxidermist, brings back from his summer holiday a long-deceased stuffed cat; De Sade, a flagellist, a cat-o'-nine-tails; Jacques, an experimental French chef, a frozen, skinned, eviscerated and headless piece of tissue, which turns out to be a marinaded cat, in course of preparation for the table; Huxley arrives with his pet cheetah on a leash. Which if any of these individuals have broken the law? Somebody has to decide, and the task is consigned to the judges in case of any dispute. Plainly merely to concentrate on the meaning of the word 'cat', as it were in isolation, will not do, for the conception of a cat is not by itself crisp enough to solve these questions. They can only be solved by reference to the context and purpose of the Act, or to some view as to what interpretation of the Act would, for one reason or another, appear to make good sense. The context and purpose may make the cases of Snooks and De Sade easy, but what of Jacques? His pussy may still be infected, and do we want to encourage this sort of thing? And what about Huxley? We might ask if cheetahs carry rabies, but this will hardly conclude the matter, for so, amazingly, do cows, and Parliament only made it a capital offence to import cats, not any old animal which can carry the disease. So any solution will be to some degree controversial; if we acquit Huxley people will say that this is silly, since cheetahs look like a sort of cat, and if we sentence Huxley to death he will protest volubly that he never brought a cat in, only a cheetah. Other words in the Act are in like case. Take the word 'cause'. Suppose a crew member on a Spanish ship anchored off Dover throws plates at the ship's pussy, with whom he has had a disagreement, and the creature, in terror, swims ashore, though it has never previously exhibited any enthusiasm for swimming. It persists in this reckless course in spite of entreaties to return from the repentant sailor. Has he *caused* the creature to be *brought* into the United Kingdom? Or is it just that the cat caused itself to enter the country in this unorthodox way? Suppose that some holiday makers, seeing the pussy in distress in the waves, swim out and rescue it, carrying it lovingly ashore and feeding it on sardines and cream to aid its recovery. Does this make a difference? Are they committing an offence?

The second reason is that the notion of a purpose underlying legislation, which may be used as a guide in interpretation, is itself problematical. In our example the purpose, as we have seen, was no doubt to prevent the spread of rabies to Britain, and this may indicate which way some otherwise tricky cases should be decided. But not always. What are we to do if the apparent purpose points to one solution, and the words to another? Suppose, for example, that there is a species of pussy, the rare Kurdish tailess cat, which is known to be wholly immune from rabies, and cannot carry it at all, but plainly is a cat. Are we to apply the letter or the spirit of the law? Of course an apparent conflict between the words of legislation and its purpose would not occur if we could, through a careful use of language, express provisions which exactly matched our purpose. But, language being what it is, this does not seem to be possible, and often the precise purpose of the law is not itself free from controversy. This may be because the legislature did not have an entirely clear purpose. In any event when a statute is drafted within a government department, and passed through both Houses of Parliament, being amended in both houses, whose purpose are we talking about? The draftsman's, the minister's, those who voted for it (many of them half asleep at the time)? So although it obviously makes sense to attend to the purpose of legislation when applying it, this will not remove all difficulties and doubts. Some lawyers have pessimistically argued that the only clear guide to the purpose of legislation is the language used, which puts us back at square one.

The third, which we have already met, is that it is quite impossible to anticipate the future with any degree of precision, so that laws have to be applied, or not applied, in situations never envisaged, and therefore never provided for, by those who originally passed them. Thus suppose we have passed laws for the regulation of ships, and laws for the regulation of aircraft – what are we do with them when the hovercraft appears on the scene? Is it a sort of ship or a sort of aircraft, or something in between? This is the problem which, as we have seen, generated the need for equity, a discretionary power to adapt the law to new situations. We do not talk of equity as such today in the application of legislation, though lawyers once did, but the point is really the same: laws are inherently imperfect, and this imperfection can only be met by the use of some degree of innovative discretionary action, action which, in the case of statute laws, is called interpretation.

The word might seem to suggest that what is involved is the simple exposition of meaning, but this is not so; nor does interpretation consist simply in the search for the intention of the legislator, as if legislating consisted simply in an attempt to communicate an intention between law maker and law applier. A better model for understanding interpretation is to think of the process of performing a piece of music, such as a symphony by Beethoven, a process in which the score and notions as to the composer's own intentions, so far as we can tell what they are, will play a considerable part. But we do not expect a musician to treat a score simply as an attempt by the composer to give instructions to all future performers as to what precisely they should do to produce the particular form of musical pleasure Beethoven had in mind when he composed the piece in question. Contemporary musical practice and conventions, and notions of musical excellence will also have a part to play, and so will the skill and mind of the performer, as well as technical changes in the design of the musical instruments now in use. An acclaimed performance will be one which strikes contemporaries, not the ghost of Beethoven, as a valid interpretation. Passing a law, just like writing a symphony, cannot be understood simply as giving a set of instructions.

The rise of legislation therefore leaves much work to be done by judges in interpreting legislation, and some theorists have argued that legislation should not attempt to give precise instructions at all; it should confine itself to general principles, leaving the judges to grapple with the problem of working out in the light of experience the precise way the principles are to apply. Much legislation is, however, not drafted in this generous spirit of trust; it goes into precise detail in order to reduce the power of the courts and enhance that of the legislature, or in reality the power of the civil servants and ministers behind the legislation in question. Problems of interpretation do not go away, and under existing arrangements judicial decisions upon the interpretation of particular statutory provisions are treated as precedents to guide what is to be done in similar cases in the future, just as their common law decisions constitute precedents, so the law that comes from statutes comes partly from the legislature and partly from the courts. This convention no doubt contributes both to the consistency of the law and to its predictability, but it does tend to have the consequence that statutes come to resemble old barnacled hulks in harbours, concealed under an encrustation of judicial decisions.

With the rise in the importance of statutory interpretation, judges and legal writers have developed theories of how the courts should approach their task, and have formulated elaborate principles and rules of statutory interpretation, which are supposed to make the job easier, and the decisions more predictable. They are set out at great length in such works as P. B. Maxwell's *The Interpretation of Statutes*. But the more elaborate these become, the less use they seem to be, so much so that one distinguished judge, Lord Wilberforce, has decribed interpretation as a non-subject. The reason for this is that not every activity in life can be reduced to rules, and interpretation is one such activity. Like painting it cannot be done well by numbers. So judges do their best, whilst oscillating between a strong respect for linguistic arguments based upon the words of the law, a strong respect for the apparent purpose of the law and a strong respect for what other judges have made of the law in question. So the correctness of particular interpretations is often very controversial.

118

LEGAL ARGUMENT AND AUTHORITATIVE SOURCES OF LAW

Law does not just happen, like some spontaneous cell mutation, it comes from somewhere. The realization that this is so is embodied in the expression 'a source of law'. We have already spoken of reports of cases, and statutes, as sources of law in this sense: it is to them we turn to discover what the law is on a particular topic. They are sources of legal information. They are also sources of law in that they record events which generated law. Lawyers and students of the law in fact use the expression 'a source of law' in a variety of different senses, and to understand how the law operates these need to be distinguished. The most typically legal sense involves the notion of legal authority.

Much of the practice of the law in courts, whether it involves pure common law, or statute law, involves argument; we think of a point of law arising in a case only when this is so, when the point is, as lawyers say, 'arguable', that is to say when a case can be made on both sides. The courts are the ultimate forum both for conducting and settling such arguments when the opposing lawyers disagree. Many of the arguments deployed in controversial cases centre in a straightforward sense around disagreement about the facts of the matter, over what happened. Such disputes have to be resolved by drawing inferences, in accordance with common sense, from the evidence presented to the court. The art of advocacy primarily concerns such factual disagreement. The good advocate so presents his client's account of what happened, and attacks the opposing account, as to make the former more plausible than the latter. Advocacy is about persuasion by appeal to lay common sense; it is however practised within an artificial legal framework dictated by rules of procedure and evidence, by conventions as to personal behaviour (English barristers have to be much more restrained than their American counterparts) and by rules saying who has to prove what, and how the matter should be settled if it is nicely balanced. Thus in criminal law the rule is to acquit unless the prosecution has proved its case beyond reasonable doubt, whilst in civil cases the most plausible side wins, even if it is only by a whisker. An example of the way in which the legal framework departs from common sense is the exclusion of evidence of previous convictions, which in common sense obviously tend to show guilt.

The dispute may however not be about the facts, but about what the relevant law is, or how it is to be applied to the facts. Suppose that it is not disputed that the accused person, who is on trial for murder, killed a security guard accidentally by carelessly discharging a gun he thought was unloaded when engaged in a bank robbery. Is this murder, or manslaughter, or no crime at all? Here there is no dispute as to what happened, only a dispute as to the legal significance of what happened, a dispute as to the law, not the facts. Legal disputes take various forms. The dispute may be very abstract, a dispute, say, over how precisely to formulate a general definition of murder. Thus in a jury trial the judge has to tell the jury what the law is in the abstract, which he does in a lecture to the jury, the direction. This has to be got right, because if it is seriously wrong an appeal court may upset a conviction obtained upon it. Alternatively a legal dispute may be more concrete, centring upon how a given definition is to be fitted to the facts of the particular case. For example, it is settled that the defence of insanity only applies if you are suffering from 'a disease of the mind'. Suppose, as happened in a case not long ago, the accused's homicidal behaviour arose because the arteries supplying blood to his brain had thickened with age, thus reducing the blood supply. Is this a disease of the body, or a disease of the mind? Odd though it may sound, some legal disputes are disputes as to whether some question of categorization is a question of fact or a question of law; in terms of a jury trial this will make the difference that the former are for the jury to settle, the latter for the judge. For example, in the law governing stealing, the Theft Act of 1968, it is laid down that only a person who acts *dishonestly* can be convicted of theft. Suppose someone borrows money from the till in a shop, against their employer's orders, in order to make a phone call home, intending to replace the money later the same day. Is it for the jury to say whether they think this is *dishonest* without instructions from the judge, or is it for the judge to say, as a matter of law, whether it is or is not?

AUTHORITATIVE SOURCES OF LAW

We have seen that argument over factual disputes appeals primarily to lay common sense (for example, a lawyer prosecuting for murder might point out that people who hide their dead wife's body at the bottom of a lake are usually up to no good). The pursuit of the rule of law, however, more or less requires that arguments as to what is the law should present themselves as appeals to the law itself. The law should surely say what the law is. In legal argument it is a quite rigid convention that argument is presented in this way, so that lawyers always argue that this or that is the law, because the law says so. The specifically legal way of attempting to persuade that a particular view of the law is correct involves an appeal to what is known as authority, which means an accepted warrant or proof that a particular proposition represents the law. The law, which as we have seen means the professional legal tradition, says what the law is by incorporating these warrants or proofs, and what counts as an authority depends upon the conventions accepted within the legal profession. They are complicated, neither wholly clear nor settled, and subject from time to time to quite dramatic change. But at any given time a body of such conventions does exist. In the common law tradition the principle authoritative sources of law are legislative enactments, typically Acts of Parliament, judicial decisions and statements of the law by expert legal text writers. So when a lawyer talks of consulting the authorities it is to collections of statutes, law reports and expert legal literature of one kind or another that he turns. They are where his warrants and proofs are to be found.

Of course the conventions within the legal profession as to what authorities exist and how they are to be used only matter because the decisions based upon them are broadly acceptable in society at large. But the public generally is only dimly aware of what these conventions are. Many people, and this includes law students at the start of their legal study, imagine that they are so organized as to make the task of courts an entirely mechanical one; all they have to do is to discover the law, and apply it. Beliefs of this kind may contribute towards public acceptance of legal decisions, but no lawyer believes life is quite as simple as that.

The way reasoning from authority works can be seen whenever lawyers dispute about the law: they try to provide reasons for the correctness of the view they put forward. For lawyers arguing a case the function of these reasons is to make their argument more persuasive to the judge. Judges, who decide the matter, also offer reasons, by way of justification for their decision, aiming thereby to persuade the legal community that they have decided aright. They do not simply give judgement like oracles, as juries give verdicts without explanation, though this practice did once exist. This is why law is a rational science: reasons are offered, or at least are supposed to exist where they are not offered, for saying that this or that proposition is a correct statement of the law. Reasons which depend upon the concept of authority may refer to some earlier statement of the law, made by a person, or institution, whose statements as to what the law is are regarded as either a conclusive argument or a persuasive argument that such a statement is correct. For example, statements of the law of his time by Sir William Blackstone, whose book on English Law, *Commentaries on the Laws of England* , I have already mentioned, are accepted as virtually conclusive arguments that this was the law of his time. Another form these reasons take involves reference to an earlier court decision, in which the same view of the law was acted upon by a judge, a person with authority to decide, in a case which is similar in relevant respects. Both sorts of reason (one involving reference to statements, the other to actions) look to what has been said or done in the past to justify what is to be done in the present. So lawyers who rely on reasons of these kinds, instead of saying 'This is the law because I say so, or because it seems to me sensible, or fair, or likely to maximize human happiness, or because I have been paid a fat fee to argue thus', instead say 'This is the law because it is consistent with what someone else, who has authority to state what the law is, has said is the law, or consistent with the way in which earlier courts have decided similar cases in the past.'

Reliance upon authority depersonalises the decision, humbly playing down the importance of the views of the person relying upon the authority. Reasoning from authority also involves the idea that the question at issue is not one to be examined as an open question, but rather one to which there is a concluded answer.

PARLIAMENTARY LEGISLATION AS AUTHORITATIVE

So far as Acts of Parliament are concerned it is a currently accepted principle of the constitution, and one which the judiciary have long respected, that the courts have no power to review the substance of an Act of Parliament and reject it as law because it infringes some more fundamental principle. What an Act of Parliament says is the law, is the law, and that is the end of the matter. Once upon a time it used to be said that statutes which infringed natural law were invalid, but this idea is no longer accepted in legal circles and is therefore not the law. So there are no legal limits upon Parliament's powers to legislate on any subject in any way, for Parliament, unlike for example the American Congress, is a sovereign legislature, not one controlled by any higher law. So courts are absolutely bound by Acts of Parliament, and what this means is that the text of an Act of Paliament is, according to legal convention, itself unquestionably the law. Judges, as we have seen, have the task of interpreting legislation, but must present their activities in a submissive spirit as never involving a challenge to the status of the text as law; this they do by talking as if they are solely engaged in a search for what Parliament really intended.

The doctrine of parliamentary sovereignty, which is the name given to the conventional understanding of the relationship between the courts and Parliament, is, like most fundamental legal doctrines, not free from difficulty. For example, if Parliament can pass any law whatever, could it pass a law providing that it was in future not sovereign? But such conundra, so like those that have taxed the ingenuity of theologians (If God is omnipotent can He commit suicide?) are perhaps more fascinating than practically significant, though there are lurking problems inherent in our having joined the European Community with, some argue, a loss of sovereignty. Sovereignty is a very emotive word.

JUDICIAL PRECEDENTS AS AUTHORITIES

The position, so far as the use of judicial decisions as precedents is concerned, is much more complex. It involves in the first place deference to hierarchy. Broadly speaking lower courts are abolutely bound by the decisions of higher courts, so that a High Court judge must accept the decisions of the Court of Appeal or House of Lords, whilst the Court of Appeal in its turn must follow the House of Lords, a rule about which it has been from time to time rebellious. The lowest of the low, such as magistrates and circuit judges, have, like so many sheep, to follow more or less everyone else. In the second place it involves institutionalisation of tradition, the past governing the present. So even the appellate courts, in particular the Court of Appeal and the House of Lords, are bound by their own previous decisions. But this is not an absolute rule, for there are some limited exceptions to the convention. Furthermore any past judicial decision, particularly one by a High Court judge, or appellate judge, is treated throughout the hierarchy as a persuasive authority. This means that it is ranked as a good but not as a compelling argument, and consequently it is acceptable to argue that a persuasive authority is simply wrong, which is not allowable, though it sometimes happens, if the authority is binding.

The use of judicial decisions as authorities is a much more

indefinite business than the use of statutes. There are four principal reasons for this.

The first is that in the case of judicial decisions, unlike statutes, authority is not attributed to the actual text of the judicial opinion. Although judicial decisions, recorded in the law reports, are used as sources of *statements* by judges as to what the law is, their status as authorities is thought to depend ultimately more on what was done than what was said. This is not the way statutes are treated. If Parliament passes a Theft Act, as it did in l968, the very words of the legislation form a basic starting point for all other argument. To be sure there can remain all sorts of uncertainties as to what the words of the Act mean or how they should be applied to a complex case, but we do at least have a text to start from, and it will often have an obvious and uncontroversial meaning. This is not the convention with judicial decisions; what is supposed to be authoritative is the underlying reason for the decision. Lawyers call this the *ratio decidendi*, the reason for deciding. Other versions of the same convention claim that, at least in the case of common law decisions, a case is only an authority for the deep principles of the law, which exists independently of the particular case, of which it is a mere illustration. A massive literature has attempted, with virtually no success, to give a crisp meaning to these ideas, which express and try to state formally the essentially imprecise notion that the law exists in the rational collective consciousness of expert lawyers, just as culture may be viewed in this understandable if also puzzling way.

The second is that whereas it is conceded that Parliament can simply invent new laws, judges, according to the traditional view of their role, are supposed to be no more than the servants of the law: it is their duty to apply law, rather than make it up. Again a vast literature exists which either claims that sense can be made of the distinction between applying law and inventing law, or that no sense can be made of it at all. But whatever the rights and wrongs of this hoary theoretical dispute, the use of judicial precedents as authorities is much affected by two further ideas which are derivative of the limited conception of the judicial function. One is that a judicial decision is only authoritative in so far as it is broadly consistent with the whole trend of judicial decisions in the relevant area of law. The second is that, since it is not the job of judges to make up law, what they say is the law in what is conceded to be a tricky or borderline case cannot be authoritative just because they say so. The authoritative quality must derive from something else, for example from the intrinsic rationality, or good sense, of what they say. From this it is tempting to draw the conclusion that precedents are only authoritative in so far as they make good sense, or, more pretentiously, in accordance with right reason.

The third is that respect for precedent in the common law system is supposed to stem from a basic principle of justice: treat like cases alike. So an earlier case is only an authority which has to be respected if it deals with a situation which resembles the present case in relevant respects. Whether this is so may, as we have seen, be very controversial. So much legal argument is concerned to argue similarities and differences between cases, and it is often possible to escape from the dominance of an earlier case whilst paying lip-service to precedent by relying upon specious or very artificial distinctions.

The fourth is that the literary form of judicial opinions is only loosely controlled by convention, and this produces rambling, long-winded and frequently obscurely expressed explanations of legal decisions. Judicial opinions, in so far as they have a standard form, are set out in the common law tradition as rhetorical arguments, just like the arguments presented by counsel to a court. The judges carry on to the bench the habit they acquired at the bar: they argue. If you go back in the law to the sixteenth century the practice was for the judges, in tricky cases, to argue the case publicly with each other, and this went on until they reached agreement. It was these arguments which appear in early law reports, which reports may not contain a statement of the eventual agreed reasons at all. Today the arguments between judges normally take place in the retiring room, and are thus private. But the convention today is to state the reasons for the eventual decision publicly, and where there is disagreement and the matter is settled by a majority the dissenting judge or judges usually explain the reasons they think ought to have determined the decision, again expressing themselves rhetorically. The argumentative form is not an ideal way of setting out a view of the law for the guidance of future courts. At their best common law judicial opinions may be elegant essays on the law, which clearly explain why the case was decided in the way it was, but many for this reason fall short of the ideal. Furthermore appellate judges do not seem to be at all good at co-operating in the production of a concise, crisply expressed summary of their agreed opinions, even if they manage to agree, as often they do not. Common law judges, raised in the traditions of the bar, are individualists, and often egocentric with it; their judicial habits are undisciplined. All this may sound deplorable, but it has a good side: the very defects of the system tend to preserve a degree of flexibility which might otherwise be lacking.

LEGAL TREATISES AS AUTHORITIES

Legal treatises, and in modern times occasionally other forms of literature, such as periodical articles, play a particularly central role in the common law system, though one which tends to be concealed. A body of law largely built up from decisions taken by the courts in real cases, and recorded chronologically in law reports, is inevitably in danger of becoming incoherent. The traditional theory of the matter is that beneath the thousands upon thousands of cases recorded in the law reports lurk deep basic principles of the common law. Cynics have sometimes wondered if these principles actually existed, or were merely a myth, purveyed by lawyers to cloak their evil activities in a veil of respectability, and pretend that the judges applied, and did not make, law. The obvious counter-move to cynicism was to say what the principles are. So, at one time, writers sought to give reality to the theory by publishing collections of fundamental legal principles, often calling them maxims. Examples include these: 'No man may profit from his own wrong', or 'He who comes to equity must come with clean hands', or 'Nobody should be a judge in their own cause'; there are hundreds of others. Often these maxims were expressed in Latin, which gave them a sort of air of deep antiquity and respectability: *qui facit per alium facit per se* (one who acts through another acts himself) or *actus non facit reus nisi mens sit rea* (it's not dirty deeds but dirty thoughts that make you a criminal). Indeed some of them are in reality very ancient, being derived from Justinian's codification. Some of these maxims are still used in legal argument and exposition by lawyers, and have become deeply embedded in the law. Their status was thought to depend upon their intrinsic rationality.

In more modern times treatise writers rather than maxim collectors have given flesh to the traditional theory of the common law by publishing in legal textbooks statements of the law, organized around general principles or doctrines, and arranged systematically, using the cases merely to support with authority what is said in the text. These books in effect tidy up and systematise the decisions of the courts, producing order from what approaches chaos; they present the cases as illustrations of the basic principles, or as deductions from them. Lawyers refer to these works in a faintly amusing way – *Salmond on Torts*, a book, it has been said, and not a savoury, or *Morris and Leach on Perpetuities*, or *Byles on Bills*, written by a Victorian lawyer who became a judge; he actually did have a horse called Bills, enabling his colleagues to remark with pawky humour, as he approached, 'Here comes Byles, on Bills'.

Such books, and other systematising works such as legal encyclopaedias, have long been the source from which lawyers have derived their knowledge of the law. At low levels of the legal system what certain books say is indeed treated more or less as Holy Writ. Examples are *Stone's Justices' Manual*, which you will see in its plastic case in every magistrates' court in the country, and *Archbold's Criminal Pleading and Evidence*, copies of which are kept on or under the bench of every Crown Court judge in the land. Only occasionally are such texts questioned or checked against the cases. However, the theory of the matter is that what text writers say is never more than a persuasive authority; the only exception, which has long ceased to matter, is Littelton's fifteenth-century work on the land law, whose very text was treated as law like a statute. Sometimes however certain passages in modern books have achieved similar status.

At one time some judges, no doubt anxious lest the text writers might rival them in status, tended to deny that text writers, apart from a small canon of writers who had held judicial office, such as Sir Edward Coke and Sir William Blackstone, were authorities of any kind. Another strange doctrine once current was that they only became authoritative when dead, and had issued their final thoughts. Once departed their rivalry was no longer feared. No doubt one reason for a rather dismissive attitude to text writers, accompanied by a reluctance to admit that their works were being used as a source of law, was that many of them were not particularly successful as practising lawyers; indeed they wrote books for this very reason.

Today the use of text writers as authorities is commonplace, and the practice of plagiarising them without acknowledgement less usual than once was the case. The extent of their influence on the law depends upon various factors. Some books acquire reputation rapidly through their sheer quality. Often however their influence develops slowly over time; lawyers, when they become important, often rely upon the books they used as students rather than their more modern rivals. Books which are first in setting out a branch of the law have a strong chance of achieving authoritative status. One very curious practice is that of keeping antique works, which have in the past established a good reputation, associated spuriously with the reputation of their original author by altering the text, whilst keeping the original author's name on the title-page. These forgeries take nobody in, but somehow retain a mysterious connection with the personal authority of the original author; they present themselves as very much part of the historic tradition of the law. One example amongst many is *Chitty on Contract*, a work written originally by one Joseph Chitty back in 1826. Joseph was gathered up to whatever heaven is reserved for special pleaders in 1838, but his name lives on. For *Chitty on Contract* is still in print in a massive multi-volume edition. This 'edition' has been produced by a large team of writers working under a general editor, and contains, so far as I know, not a single sentence written by dear old Joseph Chitty. Indeed I should not be surprised if none of the present editors have ever even seen a copy of the original 1826 edition, a fairly rare book now, much less read a word of it. The worst of such 'editions' resemble urban archaeological sites, layer of rubbish piled on layer of rubbish, and it is sometimes entertaining to track down odd sentences which survive from the earliest levels. A few years ago an 'edition' of *Stroud's Judicial Dictionary* was published which still contained some Norman French, a language abandoned by lawyers in the seventeenth century. Frederick Stroud, who had conceived a plan to unify the law throughout the British Empire by unifying legal language, had copied many entries from earlier works, including a sixteenth-century one, *Termes de la Ley*. One such entry, still in Norman French, somehow escaped the modern editor's attention.

LAW AS REASON

As we have seen, what counts as an authority (a warrant that some statement is an accurate statement of the law), and what weight is to be attached to an authority (is it binding, or merely persuasive, and if the latter how persuasive) depends upon the conventions of legal argument, typically those adopted in appellate courts. Much energy has been expended upon attempts to set out, in the form of rules, what these conventions currently are; accounts appear in standard introductory books for law students. Some legal theorists have gone farther and argued that unless there are rules of law which tell you what the law is, which enable you to recognize laws, there cannot be a legal system as we understand it at all.

Unfortunately the conventions are in many respects not clear, they do not cover all eventualities and they can change, just as social conventions do. For example, wearing a tie in a restaurant, once obligatory by convention, has become generally optional, and eventually may become quite eccentric. It is the same with legal conventions. Up to 1966, for example, it was universally agreed that one firmly established legal convention was that the House of Lords was absolutely bound by its own earlier decisions. It was legally infallible. Indeed much ink was devoted to saying what a silly convention this was. But one day in 1966 the House of Lords judges changed this; they said that in future they would be prepared to listen to an argument that they had been mistaken in the past. Since the public generally neither knew nor cared about the matter this passed with no public comment or protest to speak of, and lawyers liked the new convention better than the old one. So nobody complained and the new convention took over. So, for the reasons given, it is not possible to make any comprehensive and precise statement of the practices followed by courts in the use of authority. Legal life is not so simple.

Furthermore the conventions of the legal profession and the courts do not restrict arguments solely to those that can be supported by authority, whether binding or persuasive. Confronted with a difficult case, courts are prepared to listen to arguments supported not by authority, but by reason, and what this means is that any argument which appeals to what we may loosely call common sense can be offered to a court. Judicial decisions can be and often are justified, wholly or partially, by such common sense notions. 'Common sense' is used here as an embracing term to cover a range of ideas which form part of our shared culture, and which are regarded as providing good reasons for actions. It would be quite hopeless to attempt to provide a catalogue of such ideas, but they include moral and ethical ideas, ideas of fairness and justice, notions of practical convenience, generalisations about human behaviour or about the world we live in, as well as ideas about the role of courts in society and the limitations under which they should operate. There is therefore no closed list of the sorts of argument which can be addressed to a court.

Two examples may make this open-ended nature of rational

argument in the law more intelligible. In the famous case of *Regina* v. *Dudley and Stephens*, decided in 1884, to which I have already briefly alluded, two sailors had killed a ship's boy to eat him. They were starving after a shipwreck, and thought this was necessary to protect their own lives; believe it or not the practice was at this time regarded by sailors as the appropriate thing to do when the food ran out. Their lawyers argued that this desperate situation should provide them with a defence to the murder charge brought against them; the defence, if it exists, was called that of necessity. The boy, though courteously informed of his impending fate by the Captain ('Now Richard, your time has come'), was not consulted. In deciding that this killing was murder the court was much influenced by ideas such as these:

The weak should be protected against the strong.
The law should champion the sanctity of human life.
Extreme temptation should not be an excuse for crime.
In conditions of peril there may be a duty to sacrifice your
    own life.
Judges should not be diverted from their duty to declare the
    law by sympathy with the accused.

All these moral notions form part of a stock of common-sense ideas current in middle class circles at the time; there is nothing specially *legal* about any of them except the last. The court also thought that to allow the sailors a defence *might be a cloak for enormous crimes* (it would be too easy to lie and exaggerate the peril). This too is a common-sense idea based upon ideas about human nature. These arguments from reason were mingled with other arguments based upon authority, and the men were sentenced to death, though soon after pardoned.

Or take the entertaining civil case of *Buckle* v. *Holmes* in which the Court of Appeal had to decide whether the law governing damage done by domestic dogs should apply to domestic cats. The cat in question was a thoroughly deviant and greedy animal, which had consumed a large number of pigeons owned by a neighbour, for which it had an inordinate appetite. The court was much influenced by the common-sense idea that it would not seem reasonable to have one law for one sort of domestic pet and another for another. In the case of dogs it was settled by authority that an owner is not liable for the creature's unnatural propensities unless he knows about them; the same rule was applied to the owner of the cat in this case, for he knew nothing of his pet's strange longings. A similar line of reasoning could be applied to a cat I once owned, called 'Bushcat', which had an inordinate appetite for Callard and Bowser's nougat, which it regularly stole. Only when I became aware of this did the law require me to keep a strict control over the creature, or pay for its malefactions. The force of the argument for treating cats like dogs turns in part on respect for the value of consistency in the law, and in part on common-sense ideas as to how cats and dogs are viewed in our society. Of course in ancient Egypt, where cats, unlike dogs, were half divine, common sense might suggest a different result, for what counts as common sense depends upon social convention, and is relevant to time and place.

THE UNCERTAINTY OF THE LAW

The looseness of conventions as to the use of legal authorities, together with the open—ended nature of legal argument, and its use of common—sense rationality in justifying legal propositions, has this result, that it is not possible to state, in the form of a set of rules, comprehensive tests for telling what the law is. This means that the law is inherently to some degree uncertain, and that the process of judicial decision cannot ever perfectly conform to the ideal of the rule of law. However conscientiously dedicated to this ideal a judge may be, there just does not exist a set of tests which will, given intelligence and assiduity, deliver the uniquely correct right answer. Legal decision taking, like other forms of practical decision taking, operates within a system of non-conclusive, open-ended reasoning, which may, through its conventions, limit the range of choice open to a court but does not render it unnecessary.

Many people, including many lawyers, find this a very

puzzling and indeed intellectually unacceptable state of affairs; in consequence they have sought to develop theories of law which either minimize the problem or claim that it does not really exist. Some have argued that unless such tests exist it hardly makes sense to talk of law at all; and a well-known general theory of law, set out by H. L. A. Hart in his *The Concept of Law*, has argued that the basis of a legal system *must* consist in a basic rule or set of rules of recognition, which enables lawyers, at least most of the time, to say what the law is with some certainty. Hart does however concede that the tests do not solve all problems, but do solve many, and this is why on many questions the law is thought by lawyers to be settled and easy. But those who argue in this sort of way never actually tell us what these basic rules are with any precision at all. A recent and prominent writer in this tradition, Professor Ronald Dworkin, takes matters one step further, claiming that the law does always provide a uniquely correct solution to *all* tricky cases, though he concedes that in real life the correct solution may escape notice. He develops his myth around a super judge called Hercules, who, as described by his inventor, sets about the task of finding, lurking coyly in the legal tradition, The Right Answer To All Legal Problems. But his account of how this is done, developed with analogies from literary criticism and the writing of chain novels, though it extends over many pages of discursive text gives about as much practical guidance as an invocation to pray for divine guidance and eat nourishing meals. Its function is however not practical at all; Dworkin's aim is to develop a way of talking and thinking about the judicial process which tends to collapse any distinction between acting on given law and evolving new law out of the legal tradition. Whether this will catch on we must wait and see.

The underlying motivation for theories of this kind is to demonstrate that the rule of law is *in principle* an attainable ideal, and their authors seem to think that this can only be the case if it *could* be achieved in every case. The force of *could* here is to concede that many judges are not as good at it as Hercules, so that often the wrong answer may emerge, not the right one. The desire to show that the ideal is theoretically attainable reflects the strange idea that the pursuit of an ideal (here the rule of law) only makes sense if the ideal is theoretically attainable, as if it made no sense for an artist to pursue perfection unless he thought that perfection was attainable. Not all of us find it necessary to talk or think about ideals in this way. Saints can pursue sanctity, without thinking that it is in principle possible to become God; they hope merely to become nearer to God. Alternatively it may be that extreme idealists such as Professor Dworkin, who belongs to a long-established tradition in legal talk, find it impossible to feel comfortable with accepting law as a part of practical life. They think of law as many think of ethics, and are uneasy unless they can latch on to some objective theory of ethical truth. But law is a practical exercise, and in practical life there are often problems which certainly lack any *demonstrably* correct solution, yet have to be tackled, and it makes little difference to claim that there must nevertheless be a correct solution in principle unless there is some way of telling if it has been achieved. In practical life too we value the rational taking of decisions as a better way of proceeding than tossing a penny, even though we have, in many situations, to proceed on the basis of non-conclusive reasons. An example of such a decision is ordering one dish rather than another from a menu. There may be reasons for choosing the fish rather than the venison even though they are inconclusive and may be wrong, though if we have an allergy to venison the reason may be a very strong one.

Furthermore the pursuit of the ideal of the rule of law can be combined with an acceptance of the inherent limits in the idea of subjecting life to rules; idealism is not incompatible with an acceptance of practical imperfection. Athletes train to go faster and faster but realize they will never attain the speed of light. In practice adjudication is tolerable if it involves an acceptable mix of respect for authority and tradition, and respect for common sense, considerations which may pull in opposite directions at times. 'The law' consists of a mix of this character, and the pursuit of the ideal of the rule of law, which may conflict with other values, encourages us to emphasise the merits of con-sistency with authority and tradition, and to be cautious of imposing too much of our own personality on the taking of decisions.

Respect for legal tradition does undoubtedly produce a certain degree of consistency and predictability in legal decision, perhaps even a high degree. No doubt the conventions of legal argument, and indeed the very practice of argument, are important factors in producing this. But consistency is also brought about in more complex ways by those elaborate mechanisms which produce social conformity, and these are rarely mentioned in legal opinions. It is a familiar fact that members of professions, like members of other groups, achieve a conformity not only in behaviour but also in ideas, ideas which they take for granted, but which outsiders notice. So far as the law is concerned conformity of ideas helps to make the system operate with apparent consistency and renders it more acceptable for this reason. One powerful mechanism for producing conformity is the disapproval visited upon lawyers by other lawyers if they depart from generally held views about the law. So long as there is a measure of consensus within the legal community as to what the law is on a large range of questions, however this is produced, the claim that the system respects the ideal of the rule of law will tend to be accepted in society. This will be the more so if there is little public awareness of the degree of inconsistency within the system. This is the case, for example, with the decisions of magistrates' courts, which appear to differ widely in their interpretations of the law, for instance in relation to the provision of legal aid or the granting of bail.

NON-LEGAL SOURCES OF LAW

The title of this section may at first glance seem perverse, but once it is appreciated that legal reasoning does not operate as a closed system, like Euclidean geometry, but employs argument based upon what pass as common-sense grounds of rationality, it follows that much of the law comes from outside the legal system. Ideas which in fact influence and condition legal decision can be viewed as sources of law in what may be loosely called a causal sense.

Now one group of ideas, and a particularly important one, comprises our ideas of right and wrong and of good and bad values. In the past legal thinkers developed a curious way of talking about the fact that much law comes from moral ideas external to the law. They portrayed all rational argument which depended upon moral ideas as legal, though legal in a very curious sense. They argued that there existed in some meta-physical sense a body of law which was ideally suited to man's nature and the world in which he found himself, and they called this hypothetical ideal body of law natural law. By the exercise of reason, of rationality, human beings could think out what the provisions of natural law were, and then try to make their own law conform to this ideal system. Theological versions of this type of theory supposed that this natural law was ordained by God for his creatures. They, because they possessed some spark of divine reason, being created in God's image, could work out for themselves what the provisions of natural law were, in so far as they had not been revealed to man through the scriptures, or through the church. Secular theories of natural law would simply base the system on human rationality. The propositions of natural law consisted predominantly of what we would think of as moral propositions.

Much natural law reasoning was based upon the idea that everything had its purpose, and law which was natural would respect these purposes. This idea persists in modern popular thought, typically over certain sexual matters. For example, if the purpose of sexual intercourse is to produce children, then it is 'unnatural', and therefore wrong, to interfere with this purpose by the use of contraception. Similar reasoning outlaws 'unnatural' sexual practices, such as sodomy, which involve the use of bodily organs for purposes which are at odds with their apparent real purpose. Treason used to be viewed as an unnatural crime, since it challenged natural hierarchies of power ordained by God. There is even an Act of Parliament which treated poisoning by a cook as an unnatural crime, since it violates the very purpose of having cooks; the unfortunate cook in question was indeed boiled alive for his crime against nature. Other forms of natural law reasoning depend upon generalisations about human beings which claim that all human beings are, in some respects, naturally the same. For example, if human beings are by their very nature equal, then the law should treat them equally; this idea persists in the claim that all human beings possess or are entitled to the same rights, natural rights as they are called. So slavery may be condemned as contrary to nature, since it fails to respect natural equality. Or it may be argued that since men and women are naturally different, women should not have the same legal rights as men; this indeed used to be a common way of justifying the legal subjection of women. Natural law theories remain influential in some areas today, and the legalistic Roman Catholic Church has espoused a version of such a theory, worked out with extreme subtlety by St Thomas Aquinas many centuries ago, and little improved since. Although extensive use of the language of natural law has come to be rather unfashionable outside certain theological circles, many of the ideas involved constantly recur in moral argument today, as when people argue that some scheme of political organization, such as democracy, or social organization, such as the family, is that most naturally appropriate for the full development of human potential. And talk of human rights is today commonplace.

Other ways of talking about the matter simply say that the law is influenced and ought to be influenced by what are variously called moral or ethical or social ideas and values, and has in fact been much influenced by them. Indeed some branches of the law seem to be nothing more than elaborated schemes of morality. For example, the criminal law, at least when it is dealing with real crimes, may be seen as a legal version of the simple moral idea that the wicked deserve to be punished for their wickedness, the law of torts as a legal version of the moral idea that those who harm others ought to compensate their victims for the injuries done to them, the law of contract as a legal version of the proposition that people ought to keep their promises and perform their agreements.

A very extensive literature, much of it of a very controversial nature, has set out to investigate and construct general theories about the appropriate relationship between law and morals, theories which in earlier times would have been presented as theories about the relationship between the law of the state and natural law. Ought the law to punish immorality, even when this does not harm anyone who is not a willing participant? What morality ought the law to respect? Is there a moral obligation to observe the law even when one does not agree with it? A huge range of questions are involved here. And whether we talk in terms of natural law or natural rights, or in terms of moral claims, or ethical standards, or community values, it is clear that popular ideas of right and wrong behaviour, and ideas as to good and bad values and ways of life, have operated as a source of law in the sense that they have been an enduring influence upon the law. The in-built conservativism of the law, its respect for established tradition, expressed in respect for precedent and past legislation, may however mean that it is inevitable that the law tends to be rather out of date in its ideas. We do not look to judges as our prophets of a brave new world, but rather as protectors of past values.

The law is also influenced by other factors which have nothing to do with ethics. Public opinion, often silly and irrational, certainly influences court decisions; thus if there is a publicised belief that some form of crime is getting out of hand courts tend to inflict heavier sentences, and even to bend the law to secure convictions. A well-known example is the bending of the law in 1945 in order to justify the conviction of the Irish American William Joyce, 'Lord Haw-Haw', for treason. Joyce was a supporter of Hitler who had broadcast from Germany during the war, and had come to be regarded as something of a joke; most people thought he was British. In fact he was not, and he was convicted of treason by very tortured reasoning. He had fraudulently obtained a British passport and in theory this entitled him to the protection of the Crown; hence, so the argument went, he owed allegiance to the Crown and could therefore commit treason, which is a breach of a duty of allegiance. Of course if he had asked for protection whilst in Germany making the broadcasts he would have got short shrift from the British government, so the reasoning was pretty absurd. It sufficed to hang Joyce, and the public wanted this. More modern examples of what have been called 'moral panics' (though they have nothing to do with morals) influencing law have been the mugging scares, or the reaction to outbreaks of football hooliganism. There exists in legal circles a whole folklore justifying tough judicial behaviour which was a response to irrational public opinion, and which is supposed to have ended some grave social problem; all such stories prove on examination to be ill founded, but this in no way reduces their appeal. Some would argue that it is part of the very function of the law to give expression to feelings of public anger or concern. Others think that courts should adopt an Olympian air of detachment from the clamours of the populace.

There is also a considerable and controversial literature on the extent to which political ideas have affected the law or ought to affect it. If we mean by political ideas beliefs as to the proper distribution of power within society it is perhaps hard to see how it could be otherwise, for it is in the nature of legal decisions that they affect this distribution. Thus a decision admitting evidence obtained by the police through improper methods enhances police power and reduces the power of an accused to defend himself. A decision which allows the employer of an opera singer to obtain an injunction restraining her from singing in breach of her contract at a rival theatre plainly enhances the power of employers at the expense of employees. Virtually all legal decisions can be seen in this way; in consequence it is hardly surprising that legal decisions are influenced by basic beliefs as to how power should be distributed. If we also concede that law tends to operate as a conservative force it may not be surprising that courts tend to support the existing distribution of power in society against those who wish to change it, or who are in a disadvantaged position. It has been argued that English judges have in their decisions commonly supported authority against the underdog, the rich against the poor, the strong against the weak, the employer against the employee. If such a charge can be made to stick it does of course to some degree undercut the claim the law makes to our allegiance, and this is no doubt why writings which advance this view cause considerable unease in legal circles.

6

Lawyers

Lawyers are people who claim, frequently truthfully, to possess expert knowledge of the law, and practical skill in its working, and who earn money by selling their expertise either to the public generally, or to some particular person or institution which is prepared to employ them. There are any number of different ways of acquiring this expert knowledge and practical skill; a person with assiduity and determination could become an expert lawyer by private reading in their spare time, and some do. But the principal methods adopted in modern times, and both have a long history, take two forms: apprenticeship, and participation in formal courses of education run by law schools.

PRACTICAL SKILLS AND APPRENTICESHIP

Systems of apprenticeship reflect the fact that the law is a practical profession, like plumbing, or seamanship, or surgery. In so far as it involves a craft, the practice of which improves with experience, it can best be learnt by doing the job, though at first under the supervision of someone more skilled. Apprenticeship also reflects the fact that living law is not of mere speculative interest. Just as it is the function of medical knowledge to be used in the the aftermath of a road accident, or drunken orgy, or whatever, and not simply thought about, so it is the function of law to be applied to real life situations which are seen as problems. Now to some extent it is true that practical skills can be learnt in simulated situations; this is how much of the training of a modern airline pilot takes place. Simulators are much cheaper to run than large civil or military aircraft, and in consequence huge sums have been invested in developing them and making them very realistic indeed. Nothing at all similar has been developed for lawyers, though perhaps it might be if more effort were put into the task. No doubt one reason for this is relative cost: criminals come cheaper than criminal simulators. Consequently it is only by handling the problems of real clients that an intending lawyer can fully develop the skills involved in this process of applying and using the law. So both intending solicitors and intending barristers serve periods of apprenticeship. In the solicitors' profession they become what are known as articled clerks, whilst for the bar the apprenticeship is called pupillage.

The skills involved in legal practice are very varied. For example, a good court lawyer needs to develop the ability to present a case persuasively to judge or jury, the ability to manage and question witnesses, and the ability to cope with difficult and abrasive judges without losing his temper or making too many smart remarks, which may amuse his friends, but will risk harm to his clients. A solicitor, whose work continually brings him into close contact with lay clients, will need to develop the ability to inspire confidence in them by the legal equivalent of a bedside manner, and the ability to obtain from them, in a usable form, information relevant to the problem upon which the client is seeking help and advice. Much of what is learnt through apprenticeship does not consist in theoretical legal knowledge, as these examples show, for the successful practice of the law depends only in part upon such knowledge. Furthermore a good lawyer requires integrity; this cannot be learnt, though it is possible to give useful formal instruction on the application of ethics to problems arising in legal practice.

Apprenticeship also brings the beginner to appreciate that much of the work of a lawyer does not involve acute difficulties or problems about establishing what law is applicable to the case or problem in hand. Instead lawyers may be chiefly concerned with trying to establish what the facts of the matter are, finding satisfactory evidence, if the dispute comes to contested litigation, to place before the court, and relating what can be proved to more or less settled law. Thus in the vast majority of trials for shop-lifting no problems whatever arise over the law of theft. The question at issue is whether the accused person was really being forgetful or whether he was deliberately meaning to remove the tin of beans without paying for it. The same is true of trials for the graver crimes and for the mass of civil litigation arising out of motor accidents, an area in which it is so difficult to sort out what happened, and whose fault the collision was, that many people think it would be better to abandon the whole attempt in favour of a compensation system which did not trouble itself with so hopeless a search. Difficulties over facts and proof of facts are rendered all the more acute by self-deception, by deliberate lying and by the practice of modifying evidence dishonestly in order to make it appear more convincing, all of which go on in cases in the courts to an almost incredible degree. The practice of oath swearing, over which courts make so much fuss, appears to have not the least effect on all this.

The skills involved in good advisory work are also often only indirectly connected with legal knowledge. A lawyer consulted over the making of a will, or the handling of divorce proceedings, certainly needs to know the relevant law, but before he can usefully apply his knowledge he has first to assist his client to sort out in his own mind what he wants and what his difficulties are; to do this he needs the ability to inspire confidence and trust, and those are not skills learnt in law schools. So, paradoxical though it may seem, much of the work of a practising lawyer does not involve the use of expert legal knowledge, though much of it does, and an awareness of what the law is largely dictates to a lawyer which facts are relevant and which are not. Legal knowledge gives direction to the use of other practical skills.

FORMAL LEGAL EDUCATION

Participation in formal courses of legal education reflects, on the other hand, the fact that the law which the lawyer uses to classify and organize the messy business of life into the relevant and the irrelevant comprises an abstract body of knowledge, divorced theoretically from the circumstances which call for its application. There can be a law of murder of which knowledge can be had even if there exist no murderers and no murders. The law belongs to the world of the normative, that is it prescribes what ought to happen in certain eventualities, and does not describe what does happen. The abstract law can be set out in textbooks, and law reports, and statutes, to be read and studied systematically; it may be made the subject of lectures and argumentative discussion classes, and those who study it may be tested in their knowledge through written exercises and examinations. It is in the very nature of the formal educational course that it is somewhat remote from life and concentrates upon highly abstract and sometimes speculative issues of a type which are not the everyday fare of the practising lawyer. Furthermore the process of learning the law from a formal course can be made simpler than picking it up as you go along. This is because formal courses can be organized systematically, in a way which is entirely unaffected by the demands of legal practice. The practice of the law is necessarily unsystematic; it presents problems in a wholly random sequence as they happen to arise from day to day. Like the general medical practitioner, lawyers must cope with problems as they arise. Patients do not turn up in a neat anatomical sequence, with head injuries in the morning, neck injuries around lunchtime, shoulders next, and ingrowing toenails around midnight. Courses of formal legal education, like courses in anatomy, systematise the knowledge they purvey. So branches of the law are presented and studied as possessing a coherent structure, and in this way exposition of the law, whether by lecture or textbook, imposes order on its subject matter. Indeed the main impetus towards systematising the common law has always been the demands of education.

The distinction between what is learnt in apprenticeship, and what is learnt in formal courses of education, is not of course absolute; thus practical skills, such as public speaking, may be learnt through participation in mock trials and moot court cases in educational institutions, and so too may skill in locating legal materials through the use of library catalogues and computers. Conversely the problems thrown up by real life during apprenticeship lead to research into abstract theoretical law, and the fact that this law is going to be used practically can act as a powerful stimulus to research. Furthermore in the law, as in all learned professions, education does not cease when the initial period of training is completed. It continues throughout the whole of a lawyer's professional career, and, since the law is in a perpetual state of flux, it would be quite impossible to organize matters otherwise. Virtually everything in the way of hard information which a lawyer learns in his training becomes, sooner or later, out of date.

One skill deserves particular mention: the ability to write and comprehend the English language. A very large part of the life of a lawyer involves the use of the written language. Lawyers are forever using complex texts, such as statutes and law reports, as sources of law, drafting formal documents such as wills and contracts, or writing less formal ones, such as letters used in legal negotiations. Clear, simple, accurate use of language, together with the ability to appreciate fine distinctions in expression, are of vital importance in legal practice, and though linguistic skill can be improved in the course of formal legal education it must largely be acquired independently. Command of the language is largely related to width of general reading, and practice in writing, and low reading speed, a serious impediment to a lawyer, can be improved by rapid reading courses. They are well worth considering.

LAWYERS AS PROFESSIONALS

For there to be lawyers at all there must be a body of specialized knowledge to acquire and ways of acquiring it; lawyers exist only as experts. Closely associated with the evolution of law as a body of expert knowledge has been the development, over the centuries, of the organization of lawyers into professional groups. With the evolution of organized groups of lawyers has come the use of the law itself to support and sustain these groups. Professionalisation of the law, just like professionalisation of the practice of medicine, has meant that groups of lawyers, elaborately organized, have come to regulate and restrict the conditions in which certain legal skills can be sold.

The process involves in the first place some degree of monopoly and the exclusion of free competition in the market place. For lawyers in a court-centred system this always involves restricting the right of audience in court to members of the professional group. Thus the origin of the profession of barrister in the common law can be traced back to the evolution, in the late thirteenth and early fourteenth centuries, of a closed group of individuals who alone could appear for lay clients in the Court of Common Pleas. This group came to be the guild of serjeants at law, and was the first 'bar' to emerge in the common law system. In the second place entry into the group will be restricted, typically by insistence upon the acquisition of formal qualifications of one kind or another; hence regulation of entry is associated with regulation of education. The regulation may not stop simply at entry into the profession: a profession can be organized so that there are, for those aiming at the top, a series of filters to be passed through at various stages in professional life. The medical profession is very elaborately organized in this way, the progress from medical student to consultant involving many stages. This is also true of the legal profession, more noticeably in the case of the bar. Usually admission to the profession and progress up the ladder will be marked by rituals of one kind or another, such as 'call night' in the Inns of Court. In the third place the group will exercise a restrictive disciplinary control over the professional activities of its members. The consequence may be that members of the profession will themselves often be more severely controlled in the way in which they can provide services to the public than those who are not within it. These internal restrictions and regulations are commonly self-imposed in the sense that they originate within the group, though only from the more senior members. They will include provisions establishing professional ethics, designed to enhance the status and reputation of the professionals in the society in which they operate, and to protect the public from disreputable conduct, aims not unrelated. Some forms of purely selfish restrictive practice will come to be dignified by being treated as ethical obligations.

With professionalisation goes the development of a sense of corporate identity, and the evolution of traditional forms of behaviour, often of a highly bizarre kind, such as the wearing of wigs by barristers. Numerous professionalised groups have developed in Britain over the centuries, such as clerics, doctors, academics and service officers, and it is noticeable that their existence does not simply depend upon monopoly: in the case of the law, for example, there is nothing to stop anyone setting up as giver of legal advice for money, as do tax consultants. It is also noticeable that the professional organization of professions and its recognition and support by the state is usually justified as a mechanism for protecting the public against sharks, the element of strong self-interest involved being played down. This is commonplace with the legal profession.

BARRISTERS

Professionalisation has in England produced two surviving major divisions of lawyers: barristers and solicitors; and today when people talk of a professionally qualified lawyer they normally mean to refer to members of one or other of these two organized groups.

Barristers evolved as court lawyers, that is to say as lawyers who acted as the mouthpiece of their clients in court proceedings. Originally they were called 'story-tellers' (Latin *narrators*, Norman French *counters*); they told their client's story in court, and to this day this is their essential function. Occasionally no doubt they make it up; the late Lord Chief Justice's first Old Bailey client, when asked by the infant Goddard, fresh from his third class degree at Oxford, 'Now my man, what is your story?' replied firmly 'That's rather up to you guvnor.' Those who practised as court lawyers in medieval England in the central common law courts came to live together in fraternity houses in London when the courts were sitting there. Four of these institutions, much changed in their character over time, survive as the four Inns of Court: Lincoln's Inn, Gray's Inn, the Middle Temple and the Inner Temple. An inn of court meant a hostel for court lawyers. The lawyers who lived in them developed hierarchichal systems of seniority and government, and also organized systems of legal instruction for their younger members.

Lincoln's Inn probably derived its name from a house run by a lawyer called Thomas of Lincoln; those who lived there came to be called the society of Lincoln's Inn, and moved in the early fifteenth century into the inn or town house of the Bishops of Chichester, but kept their old name; you can still see the place name, Chichester's Rent, off Chancery Lane. The lawyers of Gray's Inn derived their name from the fact that they lived in the town house of the Lords Gray of Wilton; those of the two Temples (there was once an Outer Temple too, which survives as a name only) occupied property which had once belonged to the Knights Templar, and the circular Temple Church, though somewhat damaged in the Second World War, still contains tombs which date from its original use as the chapel of the knights, as well as the mortal remains of some notable dead lawyers. These inns or hostels, like the premises of the older Oxford and Cambridge colleges and halls, possessed the essentials of a medieval household: a kitchen, a hall with a fire in the middle, a chapel and a number of more private rooms or chambers, and their function was orginally primarily domestic. The younger members or learners, known as clerks, learnt by apprenticeship, but in time more formal education came to be provided. The systems of legal training which evolved included arguing moot cases before the bar of a mock court; a barrister was a person who took part in these mock cases. What we now know as 'call to the bar' originally was known as 'call to the outer bar' and constituted admission to argue mock cases as senior counsel from the outer end of this bar. It had, originally, nothing to do with practice in real courts. Younger mooters were called inner barristers, and the mock judges, selected from those who had given lectures ('readers'), were called benchers, since they sat on a bench.

There were originally many legal inns, some of them housing principally clerks who worked in the royal secretariat, the Chancery, and being known as Inns of Chancery. They too ran systems of legal education; none survive as legal institutions though the buildings of one still exist off Holborn, and others survive as place or building names.

The four Inns of Court of today acquired in the fifteenth century a superior position to their rivals. It is not known for certain how this came about. Probably the explanation is this. In the medieval period the job of court lawyer in the Court of Common Pleas, the most important civil court, was, as we have seen, confined to the guild of serjeants at law, of whom there were only about a dozen at any time, appointed by the Crown. All major civil litigation was handled by these serjeants, who could become enormously wealthy in consequence. The four surviving Inns came to be the only source from which serjeants were appointed, and the summit of the profession, a post as judge in the superior courts, was only given to serjeants. So to go to the top you had to join one of the four Inns. However, once you became a serjeant you left your Inn of Court and joined one of the serjeants' inns, which provided accommodation and company; these inns went with the disappearance of the serjeants in the late nineteenth century. In the sixteenth century the Inns came to monopolise admission to practise before the other superior courts of law as court lawyers; the judges would only listen to lawyers who had been 'called to the bar' by their Inn of Court. The link between call to the bar of an Inn and the right of audience seems to have been first established by the Privy Council under Elizabeth I, though not in precisely its modern form. So the Inns, governed by senior members known as benchers, came to control admission to practise as court lawyers in the superior courts, subject to a rarely exercised ultimate control by the judges. Since they could also withdraw this licence to practise by disbarring members they came to exercise a general control over barristers and what they could and could not do, and in essence this remains true today. There is no basis in legislation for the curious position of the Inns, and the historical myth of the legal profession is that it was based upon an act of delegation by the judges of their power to regulate court procedures at some murky point in the remote past.

The organization of the profession has been much modified in modern times. The formal position is still that each Inn is independent and governed by its own benchers, who have an absolute power over the admission of students and the call of students to the bar, though an appeal lies to the High Court judges. There has however been established a sort of federal organization known as the Senate of the Inns of Court and the Bar, and on this are represented the Inns and their members; this body in effect now governs the bar. It is in charge of both the regulation of practice and the educational system, operated now by another institution called the Council of Legal Education. Disciplinary cases are handled by a committee with a judge chairman, whose decision is rubber-stamped by the benchers of the unfortunate barrister's Inn. There is also an institution known as the Bar Council which goes back somewhat earlier than the Senate, and has certain regulatory powers which are subsidiary to those of the Senate.

Given the position of the Inns anyone who wants to become a court lawyer in the higher courts, which can be highly remunerative, has to join an Inn of Court and submit to the rules and regulations of the Senate and Bar Council, formally enforced by the benchers of the Inn. The top positions in the legal world, in particular judicial positions in the higher courts, have long been monopolised by barristers, as have the offices of Attorney and Solicitor General and of course that of Lord Chancellor. This monopoly over promotion to the bench originated in tradition, but has become statutory. Solicitors have, as we shall see, made some inroads into the bar's monopoly position, and it is today possible for a solicitor to become a professional circuit judge. But a solicitor cannot become a judge of the High Court. The control of the bar over judicial appointments, which are in relation to the modest attainments of many of their holders both well paid and pensionable on highly favourable terms, has become very important today. There are only five-and-a-half thousand barristers, by no means all in the running for a very large number of such jobs. So competition for them is weak; a barrister who avoids scandal and exhibits modest competence can more or less rely upon a judicial appointment in his declining years. Appointment to the High Court is a different matter; competition is still fairly strong.

Over the centuries the bar, organized through the Inns, came to establish highly elaborate systems of restrictive practices, a strong sense of corporate identity and traditionalism, a creditable if often exaggerated respect for ethical standards in legal practice and a lamentable inability to move with the times. As currently organized it cannot go on for very long, but there are at present very encouraging signs that the bar may before long put its house in order. The job of court lawyer will of course go on for so long as there are courts to appear in front of and cases to be heard, but the existence of court lawyers is not dependent upon the existence of a separate profession of barrister.

SOLICITORS AND ATTORNEYS

Solicitors did not originate as court lawyers. The name originally meant very much what we now mean by 'fixer': solicitors were a class of lawyers associated with the Court of Chancery, where they worked to speed up the conduct of their clients' cases, bogged down in the appalling inefficiencies of the clerks who administered the court lists. This was called 'soliciting causes'. Similar 'fixers' exist today in countries with corrupt and incompetent systems of administration; for a fee they will get your goods through customs, or make sure your application for a passport is considered before next Christmas. Solicitors handled business involved in the court without themselves appearing as court lawyers; in Chancery as in the common law courts this was a job done by barristers. Their counterpart in the common law world were the attorneys. Attorney just means agent, and attorneys at law were agents conducting legal business on behalf of their clients. Officially recognized attorneys were appointed to the common law courts, and they could as agents bind their clients when conducting the formal stages of litigation, a capacity in which they had a monopoly. Attorneys could get up to all sorts of knavery through misconduct in legal proceedings, and so the judges exercised control over both their admission and their conduct. There was an admirable degradation ritual when one was struck off the roll of licenced attorneys for misconduct; he could be physically thrown over the bar of the court. Attorneys, like solicitors, were not court lawyers in the sense of persons who spoke for clients in court in the course of litigation.

Both attorneys and solicitors (and you could be both at the same time) carried on a wide range of business requiring legal knowledge. This might include, in addition to out of court work connected with litigation, such jobs as drafting wills, which the modern solicitor undertakes, and also such activities as estate management and property dealing, which have come to be handled by a wholly different profession. They were generalists, and what they did was up to their own initiative in a world in which various specialisms, such as management consultants, had not yet been invented. The modern solicitor is the descendant of both the solicitors and attorneys of the past, and he has taken on functions, such as conveyancing, once performed by other professions now extinct, such as scriveners. Scriveners were letter writers, and they would draft legal documents for clients.

Some of the work which solicitors perform is reserved for them through their having acquired monopoly power. In 1804, more or less by accident, attorneys and solicitors practising conveyancing acquired their monopoly over conveyancing, though this was for long extensively shared with barristers. At the time of writing this monopoly has just been broken. The monopoly in fact covers the preparation for reward of instruments affecting all forms of property, not just land, though there are exceptions, such as wills. Another monopoly power is again of fairly recent origin, and is a consequence of the development within the bar of the rule that a barrister must not, except in some special circumstances, accept work directly from the public. So solicitors monopolise access to barristers and do very well out of this, particularly since they are under no legal obligation to pay the barristers and frequently delay payment for prolonged periods. Solicitors are technically officers of the court, and this means that their activities are to a considerable degree controlled and supervised by the judges. The *quid pro quo* is that they alone may act as solicitors and take formal steps in court proceedings, though again there are exceptions to this, for example in favour of barristers and those who litigate on a do-it-yourself basis. In outline the rule is that you may litigate in person, but only solicitors and barristers can do it for you.

Much of the legal work which solicitors undertake, such as that of giving advice on legal matters, is not protected by any monopoly power; in such areas much work which might have been theirs has passed into other hands. For example, advice on taxation law and financial management is frequently given today by professionally organized accountants and also by enterprising individuals who simply set themselves up as 'tax consultants'. The arranging of mortgage finance for land purchase, once upon a time often handled by attorneys, is now done by other institutions, such as building societies, banks and mortgage brokers. The range of legal business handled by solicitors is determined in part only by formal rules excluding others from it. Some have argued that the heavy reliance by solicitors upon the lucrative conveyancing monopoly, unkindly described by one critic as *The Conveyancing Fraud*, has encouraged solicitors to their ultimate detriment to allow work to slip away from them into other hands.

The professional organization regulating solicitors is the Law Society. Although not all solicitors belong to this organization it nevertheless is in control of the whole profession; it must be distinguished from local law societies, which do not possess the statutory powers of the national institution, and function essentially as voluntary professional associations. The Law Society proper has its roots back in the eighteenth century as The Society of Gentlemen Practisers in the Courts of Law and Equity. This was a professional organization formed to enhance the status of attorneys and solicitors and improve professional standards. In 1832 it amalgamated with a new organization with similar aims, formed in 1823 and incorporated in 1831, which became the present Law Society. In its Charter of 1845 its objects were declared to be those of 'promoting professional improvement and facilitating the acquisition of legal knowledge', objects it has indeed pursued. But like all trade associations it has also been much interested in the economic well-being of its members and the enhancement of their status, objects not divorced from each other. The principal rivals of the solicitors, and earlier the attorneys, have been the barristers, and in consequence relations between the Law Society and the bar have always been uneasy. Today the control of the Law Society over the profession is based on legislation, the Solicitors Act of 1874; its power to make regulations is subject to the control of the Lord Chancellor, Lord Chief Justice and Master of the Rolls. So the self-regulation of the profession is based on parliamentary legislation, and is partial only. Furthermore the dominance of the bar in the political world (for example, the Lord Chancellor, the Attorney General and Solicitor General always come from the bar) has meant that the self-interest of the bar in maintaining the status quo has always had a head start over the attempts of the Law Society to alter it in the interest of the solicitors. Even today there is something of the underdog about the profession, absurd though that may be. This was in the past connected with class distinctions, the bar being predominantly an upper middle class institution. The solicitors are of course very much more numerous than the barristers; there are around 47,000 of them, and unlike barristers they operate in formal partnerships. In the larger firms there is much specialization.

LEGAL EXECUTIVES AND BARRISTERS' CLERKS

Barristers and solicitors are not the only branches of the legal profession. Recent years have seen the emergence of legal executives as an organized professional group. Firms of solicitors have always employed large numbers of clerks of various levels of skill and experience. Some have carried out work such as copy-typing and filing, whilst the more experienced, known as managing clerks, occupied administrative positions of consider-able responsibility. As an unorganized group, lacking any form of professional body or trade union, the managing clerks have always been in existence in lawyers' offices, quietly conducting much legal business in the shadow of their employers. Some-thing of the order of 20,000 such individuals are currently employed upon responsible work which requires a considerable degree of legal knowledge. In recent years there was formed an Institute of Legal Executives, an organization which a large proportion of such persons have joined. It has established various grades of membership (student, associate and fellow) together with a system of educational requirements, and is currently in the course of developing into a typical professional organization. These are however early days, and it has not yet succeeded or indeed tried to acquire any formal or monopoly power. Membership is consequently wholly voluntary, though it may be encouraged by the employing solicitors. So the profession of legal executive is an existing one, but its professional organiza-tion is currently in the course of evolution only.

The bar employs its own equivalents, the barristers' clerks, who are the administrative managers of the members of the bar who have offices, called chambers, together. Chambers contain an individual known as the Head of Chambers, and meetings of barristers who have seats in chambers (that is they are co-tenants) are held from time to time, but the everyday management is handled by the clerks. Their relationship to barristers, though formally one of subservience, in reality more closely resembles that of a farmer with his livestock. Their principal functions are to act as intermediaries between barristers and their employing solicitors, in which task they negotiate the charges made by barristers for their services; and to organize the appearance of barristers in court, operating through mysterious networks and contacts which are vitally important to the barristers but largely beyond their ken. They possess an Association, but seem to be doing far too well under the existing largely customary arrangements to be in the business of enhancing their status by professionalisation. Parasitic upon their hosts, for they take a percentage of their earnings, some make enormous incomes, and young barristers live in abject terror of their displeasure.

REMOTE AND INEFFECTUAL DONS

Then there are the academic lawyers who teach law in universities and polytechnics, write books and articles about it and engage in a variety of activities connected with the law, serving for example upon law reform bodies, holding forth on television, and the like. Many of them are formally qualified as either barristers or solicitors. But although some employing institutions may require such a qualification, the profession as such remains very loosely organized indeed, and has never reached the point of laying down any formal standards of admission. Custom and tradition, coupled with the rules of employing institutions, require a first degree of good quality, and many possess higher degrees of one kind or another, but this is by no means obligatory. The level of professionalization of law teachers as a group distinct from the academic profession generally is minimal, and the Society of Public Teachers of Law confines its activities to publishing a useful directory, known in academic circles as the stud book, organizing excruciatingly boring conferences and lobbying in favour of better arrangements for legal education.

Academic law is a fairly recent development. Until the nineteenth century the common law was not taught or studied in the two English universities, Oxford and Cambridge. Their law faculties, which date right back into the middle ages, orginally taught both civil and canon law, but the study of the latter went with the Reformation, leaving only the civil law. The civilian graduates who entered legal practice worked in areas which had not been taken over by the common law, dealing with matrimonial cases, probate of wills and cases falling within admiralty jurisdiction; they had their own 'Inn of Court', Doctor's Commons. The universities of London and Oxford and Cambridge all began to develop common law legal education in the nineteenth century. With this came the invention of academic lawyers, individuals who made a career of university teaching, instead of treating teaching as merely an adjunct to legal practice. A few such academics achieved high reputation in the later years of the nineteenth century; examples are Professor A. V. Dicey, author of celebrated works on constitutional law and private international law, and Sir William Anson, Warden of All Souls and author of a best seller on the law of contract. But until very recently indeed law was not highly regarded as a university subject, the number of professional academics was small and their prestige in the main low, and not without reason. The law school was treated as the appropriate home for rowing men of limited intellect. Those going to the bar tended to read other subjects at their university, and until recently a consequence was that very few judges had ever had any regular form of legal education to speak of, the bar exams being handled by cramming institutions. The major expansion took place after the Second World War with the general increase in university education in Britain, and although this has brought an enhancement in the status of legal academics they still tend to be excluded from the heartlands of the profession, enjoying a position very different from that accorded to them in both civil law countries and the

United States, where academic law schools have long been well established.

THE FUNCTIONS OF LAWYERS

It is a mistake to think of the major division of the legal profession into barristers and solicitors as if it precisely corresponded to a division in function between different types of lawyer. To be sure barristers do monopolize court work in the Crown Court, where criminal trials take place before a judge and jury, in the High Court, where civil cases are conducted virtually always before a single judge without a jury, and in the appeal courts, the Court of Appeal and the House of Lords. Barristers may also appear in other courts; they occasionally turn up in magistrates' courts, though not in wig and gown, and in my experience as a magistrate are treated with deep suspicion when they do. But although we tend to think of barristers as court lawyers and solicitors as out of court lawyers, this is not really the position. For solicitors also have the right of audience as court lawyers before magistrates' courts, which handle 98 per cent or more of all criminal business. A large part of this work is paid for by the state in free legal aid, and although very many barristers largely live as advocates off the legal aid fund, so too do many solicitors. Those who specialize in legal aid work in the magistrates' courts perform work which does not differ in kind from their counterparts at the bar. This work is very valuable.

Legal aid in civil cases is much more restrictively limited, and the rules of legal practice in England severely restrict litigation. The loser normally pays the winner's costs, and lawyers are not allowed to take on cases on a percentage basis. Furthermore the system does not allow what are called 'class actions', in which an individual can initiate litigation on behalf of a group of people in a similar situation without their prior consent. But the solicitors have obtained a considerable share of what litigation there is. When the modern county courts for civil cases were set up in 1846 solicitors acquired a right of audience there too, and over the years this has become increasingly valuable. And even in the High Court solicitors can appear in bankruptcy matters, and in what are called interlocutory proceedings, which roughly means proceedings incidental to the main action. Before many administrative tribunals solicitors may appear as well as barristers, and such tribunals are on the increase. So barristers are not the only court lawyers. Nor do barristers confine themselves to court work. They also draft legal documents, for example complicated trusts and settlements of property, or complicated contracts; they settle the form of indictments for crime and the pleadings in civil cases; and they give advice as experts on tricky legal matters, such advice being called 'counsel's opinion'. Much of their time may be spent in conferences preparing cases for presentation in court, and in the negotiation of settlements, and this not only in civil cases. For in criminal cases very many accused people plead guilty and do not defend themselves in court, and barristers in fact, though this is often denied, take part in a form of negotiation in which a guilty plea, which saves the time of the court, is traded against understandings as to the severity of the sentence. Such a system is bound to exist since the judges encourage it by giving lesser sentences to those who plead guilty. So far as civil cases are concerned a high proportion never come to trial at all, or if they do are compromised after the case has begun, the barristers acting as negotiators for their clients. So the picture of the barrister as the bewigged hectorer of witnesses and haranguer of juries is not the whole truth.

Barristers in regular practice at the bar, of whom there are somewhere over 4,000, are curiously isolated from their lay clients, for as we have seen, except in some very exceptional circustances, they are hired by solicitors, and do not deal directly with the public. As a profession they have evolved a world of their own, and one which they inhabit in the main with much enjoyment. In addition to their archaic dress they affect peculiarities of language and court behaviour, entertainingly presented in the book *Rumpole of the Bailey* by John Mortimer. Their profession has a glamorous quality, connected with the theatrical nature of the common law trial, and barristers are still viewed by the public as somehow superior beings in the legal firmament, teeth being given to this notion by their lucrative control over judicial appointments. Intending lawyers should make an effort to take it all with a pinch of salt.

In fact many barristers do not engage in regular private practice in the courts at all. They may work as lawyers alongside qualified solicitors in the civil service, for example in the office of the Director of Public Prosecutions or in the Home Office or Board of Trade, or they may become Clerks to Magistrates' Courts, or become court officials of some other kind. Although exact figures are not known nearly as many barristers hold salaried jobs as lawyers in central and local government (where solcitors predominate) and in the business world as are in regular practice at the bar. Barristers are also to be found in academic legal jobs, where their formal qualification is functionally largely irrelevant, and in law-related occupations such as law publishing. Many qualified barristers never intend to practise at the bar or as lawyers at all, and acquire the qualification for prestige only. So far as solicitors are concerned they too perform a large range of functions which overlap with those performed by barristers. In addition to court advocacy many are engaged in salaried work in local and central government and in the commercial world, some teach, some become court officials and some may even become judges though the High Court is closed to them. Arrangements for fairly easy transfer between the two professions recognize that they do not in reality require the acquisition of skills which are not interchangeable. The fact that the division between the professions is only weakly correlated to divisions in expertise and function is one of the reasons why its continuation has long been under attack, and may well before long be abolished.

THE INDEPENDENCE OF THE LEGAL PROFESSION

The complexity of the law and the arcane nature of its procedures and conventions make it baffling and inaccessible to the lay person, and this is particularly true of court procedures. This may be experienced by anyone attending a magistrates' court and observing people attempting to represent themselves, floundering in the midst of all the standing up and sitting down, and quite unable to distinguish between the process of giving evidence and asking questions in cross-examination. Nervousness, lack of experience of the procedures and ignorance of the law combine to place such people in a very weak position indeed confronted by an experienced prosecutor. So baffling is it all that individuals sometimes leave such courts quite unaware of whether they have been convicted or acquitted.

This mystification has often been lamented, and visionaries have toyed with the idea of simplifying the law and its methods, so as to render lawyers unnecessary. But however desirable this might seem to be, nobody has ever managed to achieve such a state of affairs in any known modern society. Why this is so is an interesting question – is it simply the result of the self-interest of the lawyers? Or is it because government in modern society just is very complicated and difficult, and of necessity the process of subjecting it to rules of law is bound to produce complex law? Is law complex because life is complex? Again is it in the very nature of courts that they should be set apart from everyday life? They are, after all, instruments of authority and coercive power however they try to dress up otherwise. Juvenile courts are supposed to be 'informal', but never are. I used to sit in one in which the chairman, a highly conscientious lady, used to exude such sympathy that the children on trial were almost always reduced to sobbing and complete incoherence, and she would then ludicrously exhort them to 'listen to what the learned clerk has to say', and 'feel at home'. They knew they were not at home. Whatever the explanation, the pursuit of the ideal of the rule of law, the subjection of government to law, can have little chance of even a modest degree of success unless there are lawyers who can, through their expertise, make the law, in spite of its mystification, available to citizens. In much the same way doctors are essential if the discoveries of modern medical science are to be available to the ill.

This need for legal counsel is recognized most obviously in the free provision of legal assistance to people charged with criminal offences, particularly those which may lead to serious punishments such as imprisonment, or grave social stigma. The whole apparatus of the criminal trial is supposed to ensure that the trial is fair, that the innocent are protected, that the case for the accused is presented to the court as amply as that for the prosecution, but these things are unlikely to happen in the absence of skilled legal representation. So lawyers are needed to secure the rule of law in criminal trials; and the same is no doubt as true in civil matters, although there the right to counsel has never been so enthusiastically pursued, no doubt because the consequences of injustice there have never seemed so terrible as in the criminal law, which, at its most serious, operates by removing individuals from civil society completely.

Now respect for the ideal of rule of law is, as we have seen, a mechanism for protecting individuals from uncontrolled power; in past centuries, when government was much less extensive, the threat came as often from private power, for example from the bold bad baron, as from public power. Conditions of this kind exist at the time of writing in Beirut, a city in the grip of feuding between groups of gunmen, and one in which the law, being unsupported either by effectively organized coercive power or by general acceptance, can do nothing to prevent. In modern societies, where the state is in control, the principal threat to the individual tends to come from some organ of the state, which wants to tap our telephone, lock us up in prison or a mental institution, take our children away, appropriate half our income through taxation, deport us as an undesirable alien, forbid us to build an extension to the attic, refuse to provide us with a reliable postal service, or whatever. Where the threat does not come from the state, it may come from some other organization which has managed to acquire power supported or tolerated by the state, such as British Telecom, the trade union which operates a closed shop at our work place, or the Senate of the university to which we belong. These organizations may set about cutting off our telephone, intimidating us from going to work when there is an industrial dispute, or depriving us of the opportunity of a university education because we are supposed to have taken part in a sit-in. One form of counterbalance to the concentration of power is the existence of a legal profession, whose members are not themselves state employees, or persons in some other way indirectly under the influence of the state. Hence, it is argued, an independent legal profession is of vital importance to the pursuit of the ideal of the rule of law.

'Independence', like the rule of law itself, is an ideal, not the description of a reality. In fact lawyers, though not state employees, may succumb to various pressures which inhibit them in the degree of enthusiasm with which they single-mindedly pursue their clients' interests. A local solicitor may not be keen to attack the integrity of the local police; he has to live with them after the present case is over. Barristers who wish to become judges need to be careful not to acquire a reputation for representing radical causes; that is not the way to the top. But the ideal of independence may be partially achieved in two basic ways. One is by structures which reduce these pressures. One structure which may achieve something is the isolation of the bar from both the public and from local pressures. Another structural mechanism is the form of employment; the lawyer privately selected (even if paid out of public funds) may be less at risk than the assigned state employee. A second mechanism is ideological, and involves embodying the notion of independence in the ethical traditions established in the profession. This is the situation with the English legal profession. There is no doubt but that this may encourage independent conduct; if lawyers are brought up to believe in the value of independence, then they will tend to act up to the ideal. But one of the dangers of ideologies is that they can degenerate into myths and rhetoric; expressing them can blind us to reality. The bar in particular continually boasts of its ethic of independence, perhaps to a point at which barristers are blinded to the extent to which the gentlemanly ethic of practice at the bar tends to inhibit vigorous legal representation.

SOCIAL WORKERS OR SOCIAL PARASITES?

Lawyers, as we have had occasion to remark before, have always had a bad press; they have been viewed by many as social parasites. There are a number of reasons for this. The first is that they are supposed by the public to be themselves responsible for the very complexities which make their existence necessary, as if there were doctors who themselves spread disease and made people ill, not an impossible view of the medical profession even today. The second is that they are often thought to pursue their own interests at the expense of their clients; they are not faithful. The third is that they are greedy for money, and thus charge excessive fees if they can get away with it. The fourth is that they are hypocrites, in that the system they operate is sold as providing justice but in fact bolsters up unjust inequalities in society. The fifth is that they are pettyfoggers, who, in pursuit of their clients' interests, employ legal quibbles and distinctions which have no ethical merit, and obscure rather than illuminate the real issues involved; they pursue form rather than substance, succumbing therefore to intellectual corruption. The sixth is that they are contemptuous of truth. They will therefore defend people they know to be guilty, and advance claims they know to be lacking in merit. The seventh is that they are professionally isolated from everyday life, and thus unsympathetic and even brutal in their behaviour. The eighth is that they are excessively conservative and resistant to change; they are always out of date. The ninth is that they make money out of other people's problems and misfortunes.

All of these complaints would seem to me to be in part true; they represent statements of the way in which lawyers and legal systems in real life fail to live up to ideals which we think they ought to further. Lawyers, for example, *are* sometimes greedy; no doubt they should not be, and so on. Indeed the nine complaints listed are mostly simply indirect statements of such ideals, as is this particular example. The ninth complaint, which may be made of any profession, be it social work or dentistry, may not at first sight seem to be a statement of an ideal, but in fact it is a way of saying that charitable giving is nobler than service for hire. The so-called 'caring professions' are professions which have retained a vague connection with the notion of charity, and this enables them, in the main, to retain their caring status, a happy lot not enjoyed by lawyers or borough engineers. Since our nine complaints embody enduring ideals, and ideals are things never fully attained, there is not the least hope that some nirvana will dawn in which criticisms of this kind will cease to be made.

It does not follow that lawyers are by their very calling doomed to be mere social parasites; they can in their work try to pursue ideals of good legal behaviour. In doing so they need to recognize that they may not achieve them. Lawyers are only condemned to being placed in the same category as murderers and thieves if you believe either that law itself could exist without lawyers, which seems to me at least utopian, or if you think that the rule of law is a pernicious deception, as some Marxist-influenced radicals argue, or finally if you believe that some new form of law is possible which will escape the defects inherent in law as we currently experience it and render lawyers unnecessary.

JUDGES: FUNCTIONARIES OR HIGH PRIESTS?

A judge is a person who sits in judgement upon individuals or institutions whose legal position falls to be decided by a court. There are in fact a very large number of judges in this broad sense in our legal system. Indeed there is no limit to the number, because jurymen and women, drawn from the electoral roll, serve as judges in the more important criminal cases, deciding upon guilt and innocence. Then there are the lay justices of the peace, some 28,000 or so in all, who try the majority of criminal cases and deal with a large number of matrimonial disputes and other important business. Then there are a very large number of professional judges of one kind and another; they include stipendiary magistrates as well as circuit judges and judges of the

High Court and the senior appeal courts, the Court of Appeal and the House of Lords. Then there are a very large number of people who, though not always called judges, sit in judgement on various statutory tribunals. These tribunals can have extremely important powers; for example, the Professional Conduct Committee of the General Medical Council can end a doctor's career for professional misconduct, and industrial tribunals have extensive powers over employment relations, adjudicating for example upon allegations of unfair dismissal. So a complete list of judges would be very long and very boring and anyway nobody has ever compiled one. But what needs to be noticed is that common lawyers and indeed the public generally have a much more restricted conception of a judge than this. They usually have in mind elderly parchment-skinned creatures in doggy wigs and red robes, figures of mystery and power, whom one might meet in disagreeable circumstances if on trial for murder. These superior beings, the true judges, as it were, are the judges of the High Court of Justice, divided into the Family Division, the Chancery Division and the Queen's Bench Division. And to them we need to add the professional appeal court judges. These are the Lord Justices of Appeal, who operate in the Court of Appeal, whose effective president is the Master of the Rolls, and the Law Lords who, under the Lord Chancellor, operate in the House of Lords when it is acting as the final court of appeal. They all are in a loose sense the descendants of the twelve men in scarlet of the old system before it was reorganized in the later nineteenth century

Today things have changed. Thus there are far more High Court judges than was once the case; the present figure is well over a hundred. They are no longer exclusively male, and now include a very few women, some would say token women. For although there have been women barristers since 1919 the profession, from which all High Court judges come, is still heavily dominated by men. They are no longer quite so frightening as they once were. For the abolition of the death penalty has certainly diminished the aura of terror which once attached to the red judges who rode the circuits of the assize towns. But although real judges occupy a status in the folklore of British government which is exaggerated, they still certainly perform important functions. As well as dealing with the more valuable civil litigation, which is today carried on without a jury, except in highly exceptional cases, the judges of the Queen's Bench Division also preside over the more serious criminal trials in the Crown Court. Sitting in what is known as the Divisional Court, often presided over by the Lord Chief Justice, they also deal with certain types of appeal. And the appeal judges of the superior appeal courts handle a range of important civil and criminal appeals, the majority of which get no further than the Court of Appeal, though a few reach the most elevated tribunal of all, the House of Lords. These appellate courts sit in panels, normally of three judges in the Court of Appeal, and five in the House of Lords, which although in theory part of the legislature is in reality a distinct institution with a funny name.

The real judges of the past to a large degree made the common law through their decisions and the part they played in establishing and transmitting the professional tradition which is the law. Their decisions are to be found recorded in the law reports, and constitute a major source of law. Today the majority of the many judges who would feature in our long list do not perform this function at all; their decisions contribute virtually nothing to professional tradition. With rare exceptions only the decisions of High Court judges and above are ever reported and used as sources of law. Indeed even High Court judges only occasionally contribute to professional tradition in this way. Although there are exceptions the vast majority of the cases which form the staple food of the common lawyer emanate from the appeal courts, and since the Court of Appeal hears far more cases than the House of Lords it has come to be the most significant court in the system. Though largely reduced to the status of functionaries, whose job is confined to that of deciding civil cases and presiding over criminal trials, High Court judges still enjoy high status, and in so far as they handle very important cases, much power. This power is enhanced in criminal cases for the Court of Appeal is deeply reluctant to overturn criminal decisions from courts presided over by them. They also, given the conventions of the system, have a chance, largely denied to others, of progressing up to the appeal courts if they are lucky. For appeal court judges are only selected from High Court judges, and they are rarely appointed by promoting judges lower down the system. (A notable exception was Mrs Justice Lane, appointed in 1965 to be the first woman High Court judge; she had previously been the first female county court judge.) So although being a High Court judge perhaps no longer carries the status it once did, High Court judges nevertheless continue to rank as what lawyers regard as real judges, individuals who do not simply administer the law, but in a real sense make it what it is.

IDEALISM AND THE OFFICE OF JUDGE

Since they are the central figures in the world of the common lawyer, judges, real judges that is, are viewed with a certain degree of awe, and their doings have become the subject of a host of stories and myths and moral tales which form part of the folklore of the legal profession. There are the good judges, like William Gascoigne (*c*.1350–1419), who is supposed to have sent Prince Hal to prison for striking him as Chief Justice, thereby expressing the ideal of the fearless judge and the concept of equality before the law; the sentence was in fact pretty lenient as the regular one was to cut the offender's hand off on the spot and pin it to a gibbet. The story, immortalised by Shakespeare, is thought by historians to have no basis in fact, but I suspect it has. It is one of two stories told to illustrate Gascoigne's reputation as an ideal judge, and there must be some reason why he acquired this reputation. Then there are stern judges who do what a man has to do, such as Sir William Channell (1804–1873), who knew what to do with garrotters (as muggers were known in those days) in the days of the cat-o'-nine-tails, and whose more modern equivalent is Lord Salmon, reported in legal folklore to have ended the Notting Hill riots at a stroke by some appropriately severe sentences. Stern judges merge into fierce bad judges, such as the infamous Sir George Jeffreys (*c.*1644–1689), and there is usually at any given time one who can be viewed as one or the other according to taste, a more modern example being Sir Melford Stevenson, now retired to live in his home, 'Truncheons', who to some epitomized the ideal of the defender of law and order, especially when he locked up some Cambridge undergraduates for rioting in the Garden House Hotel there. An American equivalent is Isaac Parker (1838–1896), who turns up in Westerns as the archetypal hanging judge, always in somewhat rugged conditions in which perhaps a bit of hanging was what was needed. Inevitably he is said to have had a great sense of humour. Just to show that the law is not all boring there are eccentric judges, like Sir Henry Hawkins (1817–1907) who used to sit with his fox terrier Jack on the bench beside him, and Sir Charles Darling, who fancied himself as a wit and cracked perfectly awful jokes from the bench at which counsel dutifully laughed, and in more recent times Sir Fred Prichard, who wrote a poem about Lord Kilmuir, earlier Sir David Maxwell Fyfe, which began:

> The nearest thing to death in life,
> Is David Robert Maxwell Fyfe.
> You've only got to look at him,
> To see that life is pretty grim.

Then there is Sir Lancelot Shadwell (1779–1850) who had seventeen children in spite of a penchant for cold bathing in the Thames, from where he once is said to have issued an *ex parte injunction* to an impatient passing litigant. Lest we should forget that judges are human there have been bent judges, like Sir Francis Bacon in the seventeeth century, who took bribes, and in the eighteenth century Lord Macclesfield who got into embarrassing financial difficulties associated with the South Sea Bubble. As for sexual irregularities there is the celebrated lecher Sir John Willes (1685–1761) whom you may see resting from his exertions in Hogarth's ferocious painting 'The Bench', now in the Fitzwilliam Museum in Cambridge.

To redress the balance again there is a whole canon of great and learned judges, who are thought to have made outstanding contributions to the development of the learned profession of the law. They include Sir Edward Coke (1552-1634), a major political figure too, of whom his wife said when told of his death: 'We shall never see his like again, praise be to God', and Lord Mansfield (1705-93), one of whose houses, Kenwood, you may visit in London (it contains notable paintings by Stubbs, Vermeer and Rembrandt), though his central house was burnt down by the mob in the Gordon riots and is no more. For the nineteenth century there is a considerable list of contenders, of whom perhaps the most notable and entertaining was Baron Bramwell (1808-92), a rugged individualist if ever there was one, and more recently in this century the bearded Sir Thomas Scrutton, master of commercial law, whose abrasive manner made him too many enemies to ever make it to the House of Lords. And as for saints, the common law has produced only one in the religious sense, Sir Thomas More, but in recent times Lord Atkin (1867-1944) has for many lawyers come to occupy a similar role. He is famous for his opinion in *Donoghue* v. *Stevenson*, the case of the snail in the bottle. In it the plaintiff claimed to have been made ill by the snail, which had decomposed, and sued the manufacturer of the ginger beer in which the creature had gone to its penultimate resting place, and Lord Atkin's opinion has become the basis for the modern law of compensation for negligent injury, though some doubt exists as to whether there ever was a snail in the bottle. He is also one of the only two judges who made any fuss at all about the locking up of British citizens without trial in the Second World War. Of contemporaries Lord Denning, not long retired from the office of Master of the Rolls, to many epitomises the best sort of judge, but it is perhaps early days to say more.

We may view many of these stories about judges, be they fact or fiction, as reflecting attitudes to the office of judge and the ideal picture of those who should occupy it – fearless, stern, human, uncorrupt, wise, even saintly. Some would add creative, but at once we are involved in a contradiction, for the ideal of the rule of law requires the judge to be simply the servant of law, a mere functionary, and in so far as we admire a judge who creates law we are obviously departing from that ideal, here as elsewhere in life exhibiting a curious inconsistency. Of all the values associated with the office and its function in government under the rule of law the most valued is that exhibited by William Gascoigne – independence. To this end judges of the High Court and above are specially protected from dismissal under our con-stitutional arrangements, and although quite a number of judges have in fact been eased out of office by pressure, sometimes justified by their senility or bad behaviour, no real judge has actually been formally sacked since the modern arrangements were set up in 1700. So judges are fairly effectively protected from crude political or executive pressure to give decisions favoured by government. How independent they are from more subtle pressures is more of an open question. The formal arrangement cannot insulate judges from such pressures as the approval or disapproval of their colleagues, and the system of promotion to the Court of Appeal and beyond, which is under Cabinet control, encourages a level of conformity to the wishes of government which can be sinister. So the ideal of indepen-dence, like other ideals, may not be perfectly realized, but remains nevertheless a powerful feature of the ideology of the legal profession.

7

The Academic Study of the Law

Systems of formal education, and legal education is no exception, always involve a considerable degree of compromise. We have already seen how, for a lawyer in practice, legal education is in a sense a permanent condition. The law is forever changing and developing, and even if this were not the case the demands of practice will continually force a conscientious lawyer into grappling with new problems, for which his existing stock of knowledge may be inadequate. But courses of formal legal education cannot be prolonged indefinitely; they can only be allocated a limited period of time, normally three years, and this imposes severe constraints upon what subjects may be studied, and in what detail. So the end product is always something which everyone agrees is a compromise between depth and coverage. So far as coverage is concerned a combination of pressure from the organs of the profession, together with an uneasy consensus amongst legal academics, has meant that all specialist degree courses are dominated by the study of the so-called 'core subjects', to which is virtually always added some form of introduction to law. This may be largely historical, or it may concentrate more modestly, if boringly, on purveying basic information about the structure and organization of the legal system. Or it may be highly theoretical, aiming to explain how lawyers think and reason, or how law functions in society, and what effects it has; again the end product may represent a compromise. This all leaves only limited room for the study of further subjects, and these, following a slightly frivolous terminology, may be divided into 'useful' and 'useless' subjects. The former comprise branches of law currently in operation in the English legal system. Examples are Family Law, Company Law, Tax Law, the Law of Evidence, Welfare Law, the Law of Civil or of Criminal Procedure, the Law of the European Community, Private International Law (also, as we have seen, called Conflict of Laws). All these branches of the law have an obvious practical relevance to the work of an English lawyer. To this representative list we could perhaps add Public International Law, for this is a system currently in operation, and has its specialist practitioners, though most students who opt for it do not in fact do so with a view to using their knowledge directly in legal practice

The 'useless' subjects are those not immediately relevant to legal practice; they include Legal History, Comparative Law, courses involving the philosophical study of law, variously called Jurisprudence, Legal Philosophy, or Theory of Law, Sociology of Law, Criminology and Penology, and branches of ancient Roman law, for example the Roman Law of Sale, or of Contracts. Roman law may be studied as providing an introduction to the system of legal thought which is typical of civil law systems, such as are all the systems of continental Europe. The relevance of such 'useless' courses to formal legal education is thought to lie in their capacity to enhance understanding of legal development and the functioning of law, and, it can be argued, this understanding is, in the long term, of practical value. Alternatively their claim to be included may be thought to lie solely in the intellectual interest in seeking solutions to the problems of understanding to which such courses are addressed.

What courses are offered beyond the 'core' courses, and how much time is allotted to 'useful' and 'useless' options, will depend upon the resources and interests of particular law schools, and the compromises reached in allocation of time and people. But whatever form the eventual curriculum takes any system of legal education is confronted with certain intractable problems which reflect differences in attitudes both to the function of legal education and the nature of law itself. These differences give rise to what may be viewed as the dilemmas of legal education, and as such they have no clearly correct solution.

DILEMMAS OF LEGAL EDUCATION

Everyone agrees that the education and training of lawyers should involve the acquisition both of legal knowledge and of legal skills, though precisely in what mix, or in what ways, remains somewhat controversial; some of the skills involved are no doubt more easily learnt through apprenticeship, though many of the conventions of legal argument and methods of analysis can certainly be taught before apprenticeship begins. But not everyone who takes a formal law course intends to enter legal practice, or will in fact end up in practice, and so there is, for this reason alone, a feeling that legal education should, like other forms of higher study, provide something in the nature of a general education, an aim which can obviously conflict with the demands of a severely practical and professional approach to legal study. Furthermore there is no doubt but that the law can be taught, albeit somewhat crudely, as consisting in nothing more than a set of rules to be memorised. But this way of presenting the subject is intellectually uninteresting, distorts the character of the subject and seems to contribute little to understanding law and the way it operates. All this presents legal education with a dilemma of choice between two antithetical approaches to legal study. One approach emphasises the professional, practical aim of equipping the intending lawyer with information and skills of a type which appear immediately relevant to the practice of the law. This approach will usually be associated with a process of education which in some sense indoctrinates the student with the conventional wisdom and attitudes of professional lawyers. An opposing approach will instead emphasise theoretical understanding of the phenomenon of law. It will seek to investigate, for example, the way law develops and operates in our society and may even be said to create, at least partially, the world we live in. Its aim is not that of equipping intending lawyers with a basic information kit.

Another way of characterising this dilemma is to see in it a choice between aiming to insert the student of law into the professional tradition, and aiming to stand outside the legal tradition and be the uncommitted observer of it. We might contrast the two approaches, albeit somewhat tendentiously, by calling one that of legal indoctrination, and the other that of clinical observation. But of course law is not like a rabbit which one can catch, put in a box and study whilst remaining wholly unrabbit-like oneself, or like a battle you can watch from afar through binoculars without becoming involved in it. You can only usefully study law if you have in some sense learnt what it is to be a lawyer, so that some involvement in the more traditional professional approach is a necessary prerequisite to anything more sophisticated. It is idle to have bright ideas about the social significance of the law of homicide without having acquired some level of knowledge and professional understanding of what it is. This presents a practical problem over the allocation of time, and a deeper intellectual problem, in that too professional an education can inhibit the ability to stand outside the system and treat it as an object of study. The same sort of problem confronts social anthropologists, who have both to join the alien culture which they wish to study and somehow try not to let it take them over completely, so as to deprive them of the opportunity to observe it.

A second dilemma arises in the following way. Given the imperfections of the law, reflected as we have seen in the criticisms constantly directed both against the law and its practitioners, everyone would also agree that legal education should be critical, that is to say it should encourage the law student to question the merits of the system as it exists and works. Indeed even the most hidebound lawyers and legal educators have conceded this much, and a traditional activity associated with legal education has been an interest in improving the law. One form this may take is by rationalizing and systematising the law, and this has long been work in which law teachers have been engaged. Another activity is called law reform, and consists in taking the existing law, identifying what are seen to be defects in the way it operates and suggesting ways in which the law may be amended. In countries like the USA where the operation of the doctrine of precedent has somewhat broken down under the sheer mass of reported cases, and courts are more prepared to intervene actively in law reform, law reforming activity may be directed at courts, whereas in England they may be directed more at Parliament. A critical approach to the law expressed in ways such as these is in no sense radical, for its quarrels with the law go only to matters of detail.

But the dilemma arises because criticism can go much deeper. It may involve questioning fundamental assumptions which go to the root of the operation of legal systems. For example, take the ideals traditionally associated with legal practice: perhaps the rule of law is indeed a pernicious myth, as some radicals claim. Perhaps the system is in reality dedicated to injustice, not justice. Perhaps the whole notion of guiding human conduct by rules is incoherent and senseless. Radical criticism of law, developing ideas such as these, may more or less come round to the view that law is not a good thing, but a thoroughly bad thing, or perhaps just a delusion, and this extreme radicalism or scepticism does present legal education with a dilemma. Imagine a medical school dedicated to teaching its students that in a quite general way doctors were bad for your health, or a theology faculty engaged in convincing its students of the truth of atheism, or of the idea that God was dead. Radical criticism seems impossible to reconcile with any conception of legal education as professional education. Indeed traditional forms of legal education may be viewed by a radical critic as themselves part and parcel of the mechanisms which maintain injustice and oppression in society. But perhaps the radicals are right, and if legal education is to be viewed as intellectually respectable within universities as we understand them it cannot shrink from the pursuit of truth simply because the truth is institutionally embarrassing, or refuse to consider ideas because they are subversive. In the world of scholarship there cannot be a list of views which one is not allowed to put forward and examine simply because they are unpalatable to the legal profession.

A third dilemma can be presented in the following admittedly simplified way. In general the scholars who work in universities and other places of higher learning are engaged in the search for truths of one kind or another. Thus historians are busy trying to find out what happened in the past, and economists are busy trying to formulate propositions about the way in which economic laws operate in society, and so forth. The various disciplines all claim to have some form of truth which they are investigating, and often combine this with the claim that they involve some distinct method of enquiry; whether this is so is the subject of a considerable philosophical literature. But it is not easy to see that the law itself is a discipline in the usual sense. What truths do lawyers as such come up with? What are the great legal discoveries of the past ten years, or fifty years, or even a hundred? There do not seem to be any. Hence some feel that legal education, if it has any right to exist in places of higher learning, rather than in trade schools, must involve the application of some distinct discipline to the law as an object of study. For example, we might apply economic theory to the law, or sociological theory, or study the historical evolution of law, or apply philosophical ideas to the law. But once we start on this road it is not clear that law itself remains a subject in its own right at all, and that is hardly a palatable conclusion for legal educators and legal education, nor is it a conclusion easy to reconcile with the conception of legal education as professional education. So there is a tendency to try to escape the dilemma by compromises, in which insights from other disciplines are as it were slipped into law teaching *en passant*, or by adopting what has been called the 'Law and . . .' approach, running courses on Law and Psychology, Law and Economics, Law and Social History; both forms of compromises run the danger of that superficiality which is always a risk in interdisciplinary work. Of course the dilemma under discussion only arises if you adopt an attitude to the function of higher education which may be summed up in the expression 'the disinterested pursuit of knowledge for its own sake'. If you think that understanding is another acceptable commodity then legal study does not seem so out of place.

Attempts to resolve these dilemmas would be easier were not life short and the time allotted to legal education necessarily limited, and a very theoretical approach easier to sell if it were not the case that so many of those who undertake courses of legal education are primarily interested in making themselves into competent lawyers; they want to join the system, not question it or indeed, a cynic might say, understand it. Given limited aims they have a point which has to be conceded, for what it is worth, and it is this. It is indeed perfectly possible to rise to dizzy heights in the legal profession whilst possessing perfectly childish notions of how the law affects real life or being wholly uninterested in the matter. It is an article of faith amongst academics, who are by nature worrying introspectives, that this somehow ought not to be the case, but I fear it is.

DOCTRINAL LEGAL STUDY

Traditional academic legal education concentrates upon the study and analysis of legal doctrine, and upon the application of legal doctrine to given factual situations. All law schools, whether or not they claim to be at the innovative or radical end of the spectrum of legal education or not, devote much effort to this form of academic study.

Doctrines consist of traditional ways of analysing situations which give rise to legal problems, and traditional ways of solving them. For example, suppose that someone who has lost a pet dog advertises the fact, and in the advertisement says that a reward of £2,000 will be paid to anyone who returns the dog. Our problem is to determine whether this advertisement can give rise to a legally enforceable obligation to pay the reward to the finder, our client, supposing that the dog has been returned and payment refused. This looks like a problem in contract law, contracts being what lawyers call agreements, but the catch is that there has not been an agreement here in any everyday sense, just a one-sided promise; our client never met the dog owner in his life before he returned the dog. However, it is a doctrine of the law of contract that a promise or undertaking is binding if it is supported by 'consideration', and consideration can consist in a reciprocal promise, or in an act. So that suggests that, although in this instance there seems to be an undertaking on one side only, there may nevertheless be a binding contractual obligation on the owner. Another aspect of the doctrine of consideration is that an act which is to count as consideration (here returning the dog) has to be something of benefit to the person making the promise, or giving the undertaking, or something which the actor is not legally bound to do, and therefore in some sense a detriment to him. Returning the dog would seem, according to this doctrine, to be home and dry, and so the finder, our client, is entitled to the reward.

But suppose the dog is decrepit, smelly and repulsive in its habits, and worth virtually nothing; indeed most people would need paying to keep it. Does this matter? Does it matter that the reward is quite out of proportion to the value of the dog, or the effort involved in returning it? Here another aspect of the doctrine of consideration seems to help. It is part of the doctrine that courts do not enquire into what is called the 'adequacy' of consideration, so the legal answer is that it does not matter. Here of course common-sense views of fairness might take a different line; indeed some people would regard this as a gift promise anyway.

Now let us suppose that the owner in fact was delighted to lose the dog and put the advertisement in as a joke, never imagining for one moment that anyone would take the promise of so large a reward seriously. Here another doctrine of the law of contract seems relevant: it says that promises are only binding if they are seriously intended. At first sight this seems to favour the owner, but wait a minute; another doctrine says that when matters of intention are involved we attend not to the promissor's actual intentions, but rather to the intention a reasonable person would attribute to him on the basis of his actions, here the

180

action of advertising the reward. So probably a court would say that a reasonable person, seeing such an advertisement, would suppose it to be seriously intended, and consequently rely upon it. But if the finder concedes that he thought it was a joke the position might be different.

Now suppose we alter the facts slightly, and suppose that the advertisement was not seen by our client until several days after he had returned the dog; he knew who owned it and just acted out of kindness. Can he now claim the reward? There are various doctrines of contract law which might seem to help, but it is not very clear how they should apply to such a puzzling case. Thus one doctrine analyses all contracts into an offer (here the advertisement) and an acceptance (said here to be the returning of the dog). But does it make sense to say that you can accept an offer you have never heard about? Another doctrine says that if something is to count as consideration it has to be given 'in return' for the promise. Well, returning the dog is what the dog owner wanted in return for his promise, but when the dog was returned the finder did not return it 'in return' for the promise, but out of the kindness of his heart. So whereas our earlier problems seemed fairly easy to resolve through applying legal doctrine, this last case seems to raise questions about what the law of contract is all about. If it is there to protect people who have acted as they did in reliance upon other people's promises, the dog finder ought not to be protected here. He did not rely on the promise when he returned the dog. On the other hand, if we think it right that the law of contract should hold people to performing promises to pay for actions so long as the conditions they have attached to the promise have in fact been fulfilled, then the promise should be binding. A purely doctrinal approach to this conundrum will take the form of trying to see which solution seems most consistent with earlier cases dealing with the formation of contracts and with the reasoning used in them, and also most obviously rational. One line of reasoning might involve trying to show that underlying the mass of cases on contract law was a basic idea: that contract law was there to protect legitimate expectations aroused by promises. It would follow from this that you cannot in law accept an offer you have never heard of, and thus the dog finder would lose his case.

Legal doctrines pass under a variety of names. Sometimes lawyers talk of principles of law, meaning by this legal propositions of a fairly high level of generality which have a capacity to point to appropriate solutions in a wide variety of situations. For example, the sovereignty of Parliament is a principle of the British Constitution, and from this it seems to follow that whatever Act of Parliament you come across, and there are thousands of them, it is never legally correct to decline to accept the Act as law on the ground that Parliament had no legal right to pass it. Parliament can pass any law it likes. Some principles have traditionally, as we have seen, been embodied in Latin tags, called maxims. Thus in criminal law it is a general principle that *actus non facit reus nisi mens sit rea*. This tag is virtually impossible to translate literally, but the force of it is that what a person does by itself does not make him a criminal unless he has a criminal state of mind, or, more simply, that criminality lies in the mind rather than in the body. So, for example, if I pick up your umbrella this is not theft unless I knew it was yours, and dishonestly meant to keep it. On the basis of this principle criminal lawyers have built up an elaborate analysis of the nature of serious crimes which divides the requirements which have to be proved into an *actus reus*, an act forbidden by the law, and *mens rea*, meaning the appropriate attitude of mind which must exist if a crime is to be committed. This analysis can also give rise to conundrums. For example, it seems to be obvious that the criminal act must be something forbidden by law. Now suppose an executioner hangs someone who has in fact been sentenced to death, and whom it is his job to hang, but he does not at the time know this; he just likes hanging people. Does it make sense to say he is innocent of murder because what he did, his act, was not against the law? Do we want to have executioners hanging people at random and getting off if they are lucky enough to pick on a convicted criminal? So something is amiss with our apparently sensible analysis.

Legal doctrines are also called rules, especially if they are fairly specific and crisp in the guidance they give. In the law of murder it is a rule that the death must occur within a year and a day of the criminal act for the death to be regarded by law as caused by that act. Again the term rule is often used when a precise verbal formulation of the doctrine has come to be accepted within the profession; rules are often associated with cases which established such a formulation. So the 'M'Naghten Rules', which deal with the defence of insanity in criminal law, were formulated very carefully by the judges in 1843 in response to questions put to them by the House of Lords; the exact text of these rules has become part of established legal tradition. Doctrines also take the form of definitions (murder in law means unlawful killing with malice aforethought) and distinctions, and will be found sometimes given other titles, such as 'fundamental assumptions', 'legal presumptions' and numerous others. All are doctrines in the sense that they are part of the special learning of the profession whose function it is to provide an analysis and way of resolving legal problems.

Doctrinal legal education in the common law world is everywhere typically casuistic; it concentrates upon the analysis of tricky borderline cases where either the legal tradition or common-sense rationality, or both, seem to pull in opposite directions, or provide no clear guidance as to how the matter should be settled. These cases may be real ones. Take for example the entertaining case of *McQuaker* v. *Goddard* which arose out of an incident in which a visitor to a zoo was bitten by a camel. Now the legal tradition, embodied in case law, made a distinction between liability for injuries caused by wild animals (animals *ferae naturae* in legal jargon) and injuries caused by domestic animals (*mansuetae naturae*). The owner of a domestic animal was only liable if he was negligent or knew of the vicious propensity of the creature, as he would do if this was the second bite. But it was not. However, for wild animals there was no need to prove negligence or knowledge, for the owner was liable strictly without any proof of fault being necessary. So much was settled law, but into which category ought camels to be placed? Plainly much may be said on both sides. In Britain camels are not kept as domestic pets or farm animals; they are found only in zoos, and they are creatures of perfectly appalling habits, as anyone who has tangled with a camel knows. On the other hand, camels of the type in question are nowhere found living wild, except perhaps when they have escaped and as it were become feral camels, and they have long been domesticated in desert regions. Indeed a camel drover was produced to the court who claimed that they are so dependent upon man as to be incapable of copulating without human assistance, a tale which is I suspect a Bedu joke, but was taken very seriously as a piece of zoological information of critical importance by the judges who had to decide the case. They plumped for the view that they were in law domestic animals, so the plaintiff lost the case.

Now a case involving a tiger would raise no intellectual difficulty; in terms of the legal tradition it is plainly a wild animal. But the case of the camel, being on the borderline, forces us to examine very carefully precisely what the basis of the distinction ought to be, and, indirectly, what the point of it is. Should the distinction turn upon whether the animal is of a type normally kept in this country only as a domestic or farm animal? If so, then presumably at a time when mink farming was common mink would count as animals *mansuetae naturae*. Or should it turn rather upon whether the animal in question belongs to a class of animals which are both kept as domestic or farm animals, and are in general not dangerous? And when we say dangerous do we mean dangerous to man or to other animals, or both, or either? Should the relevant principle be that in order to count as an animal *ferae naturae* a creature must, at the least, be found somewhere in a wild state? Of course if we say this, and all the wild gorillas die out, so that the only stock exists in zoos, gorillas will become animals *mansuetae naturae* at the moment when the last free-range gorilla dies, which seems faintly absurd. So a case like the case of the camel serves the function of concentrating the mind on the precise formulation of the distinction, and the common-sense reasons for it, if any there be. And real cases, like this one, can easily be modified to produce other hypothetical borderline cases which serve the same function. What, for example, should be the legal status of the hamster, which certainly does bite? And what should we say about some exotic pet animal of a wholly benign character, such as a fruit-eating spider of alarming appearance which escapes and causes panic leading to a broken leg? And so on. Lurking behind the somewhat hair-splitting arguments which are deployed on the borderline will be ideas about what sense, if any, it makes to have two rules of liability for injuries caused by animals and not just one. So a doctrinal study of the law will often involve attempts to formulate and make sense or nonsense of the underlying rationale of legal rules and doctrines, for they are supposed to rest not just on authority in the form of earlier precedents, but also in part on reason.

Doctrinal legal education in part simply transmits knowledge of legal source material; having studied the case of the camel a student will at least know that the Court of Appeal did rule, back in 1940, that camels were in law creatures *mansuetae naturae*. But this is not really its purpose. Instead this is often said to be that of teaching students to think like lawyers, and what this in fact means is to familiarise themselves with the sort of reasoning employed by courts, and the conventions followed by them, in dealing with cases which generate some level of controversy about the state of the law. So doctrinal legal education is parasitic upon, and imitative of, court reasoning, and takes decisions recorded in the law reports as its principal model. To a lesser degree doctrinal legal education is modelled upon the conventions followed by legal expositors, who set out to systematise the law in legal textbooks, and here the emphasis is not so much upon the individual tricky case as upon the presentation of a branch of the law as a consistent and systematic whole. But again the forms of reasoning according to which propositions are supported are modelled upon the reasoning of courts, particularly of course appellate courts, where the most skilfull judges deploy their considerable powers upon tricky questions. As we have seen, court reasoning is conventionally justified partly by an appeal to the legal tradition through the use of precedents, partly by reference to authoritative texts and partly by an appeal to common-sense ideas, that is to rationality. Doctrinal legal education employs these forms of justification too.

THE ASSUMPTIONS OF LEGAL SCIENCE

Doctrinal study of the law proceeds on the underlying assumption that the law can be set out in the form of a consistent body of principles, rules, definitions, exceptions, et cetera, which can be applied to factual situations so as to generate a single legally correct answer to the problem presented for decision, whatever that problem may be. Built into this assumption is first of all the notion that the law is all embracing; there are no legal questions to which there are no legal answers. We might ask some such weird legal question as this: 'Is it a crime to hate hamsters?' The law gives an answer even to so weird a question as this; the answer is 'No'. Of course it has to be a legal question; the law has nothing to say about whether hamsters make good pets. Also embodied is, second, the notion that the law must always be consistent, so that it cannot both be a crime and not be a crime to hate a hamster. It has got to be one thing or the other. A further curious assumption is that legal propositions are timeless, just as moral propositions are timeless; it hardly makes sense to say that murder is wrong, or a crime, today, but may not be tomorrow. This way of looking at the law conceives of the law as a comprehensive science of proper social relationships, and has long dominated legal thought. It is the traditional way in which courts and professional judges have always looked at the law, and it is integral to doctrinal legal study which is, as we have seen, imitative of court practice. According to legal science the job of the expert lawyer is that of discovering what these principles, and so forth, are, formulating them accurately and applying them properly to the facts of cases. In much the same way a doctor's job might be viewed as being that of discovering and applying the principles of scientific medicine to his patients. Victorian lawyers did indeed often compare their work to that of the natural scientists. The belief in legal science was compatible with notions as to division of responsibility. Judges, for example, had to be good at application, but they might be helped if theoretical writers (the equivalent of medical researchers) worked out the principles for them and set them out in books. Academic legal education could be viewed rather mechanically as the business of teaching students what the principles are, and giving them practice in applying them, or as a more intellectually exciting enterprise of teaching them how to become legal scientists themselves in their own right, just as education in the natural sciences can be viewed in either of these two ways. A famous Dean of the Harvard Law School, who was, believe it or not, called Christopher Columbus Langdell, thought that with a little guidance the law student was capable of discovering the principles for himself, and based a whole system of legal education upon this optimistic belief. A belief in legal science is perfectly compatible with the notion of error; judges can get things wrong, and so can anyone else. But it involves the claim that they can get it right, because there is a right and a wrong, a correct and an incorrect answer to all questions. We have already met this idea and seen that it is connected with the idealism of the theory of the rule of law.

Now all doctrinal legal reasoning is carried on as if the assumptions of legal science are correct. For example, in a court barristers do not ever get up and say to the court that the problem involved in their case is one to which the law provides no answer, so that, as lawyers, they have nothing useful to say and might as well sit down. Nor do judges ever explain that the law provides two contradictory answers to the case, and since it is Tuesday they will go along with Answer A (this is a crime), but had it been Wednesday they would have given Answer B (it is not a crime).

As we shall see, many people nevertheless think that the assumptions of legal science are in some sense myths, things that in the law we pretend to be true although we know that they are not. They think that the law does not really provide one single correct answer to every question, or alternatively that there is no real way of showing whether it does or it does not. But even if this scepticism is justified, it is nevertheless difficult to see how doctrinal legal argument could possibly be conducted at all unless the assumptions of legal science were accepted at least as conventions as to how we argued about the law. How could one conduct a legal argument on the basis that both sides of the argument could be right at the same time? Or on the basis that the first question to settle was whether there was a correct legal answer to the problem, and if there was not, then the second question would be to settle the form that a non-legal answer would take. If the assumptions of legal science are myths, they seem to be useful myths that make law and legal argument as we understand it possible. This is perhaps why in the doctrinal study of the law, even when it is conducted by people who consider the assumptions of legal science as in some sense untrue, legal problems are always discussed as if it were possible to tease out of the legal sources a correct answer to the problem. Similar assumptions underlie other forms of practical rationality.

The doctrinal study of law, with the underlying theory of legal science, has come in for a great deal of criticism, and as we shall see a whole school of thought has developed in opposition to it. It is often spoken of in a dismissive way as involving no more than a memorisation of legal source material, called 'black-letter law' because back in the old days law books were published in a gothic type-face known as 'black letter'. But this is not in fact the case, for doctrinal legal education is concerned with argument and analysis, not with memorisation, and concentrates as we have seen on situations in which there is usually no obviously correct solution to memorise. It is also sometimes attacked upon the ground that it is uncritical, but again this is not really true, though the forms of criticism involved are confined by the conventions of legal argument. Another form of objection is that the effect of doctrinal legal education is to encourage what is often called a formalistic approach to the law, in which solutions to legal problems are presented as the inevitable deductions from legal doctrines derived from precedent without attending to notions of purpose or function, or to the need for the law to keep up with the times. No doubt this can be so, but at its best doctrinal legal study will attend to these matters; it all depends upon who is running the course. Indeed traditional doctrinal study can be used as the vehicle for showing that the assumptions of legal science are myths.

LEGAL REALISM AND MODERN ICONOCLASM

Iconoclasts are people who attack and destroy icons, sacred things, and there have always been individuals who have adopted an iconoclastic attitude to the sacred things of the law, in particular the concept of the rule of law. There is indeed a medieval case in which the opposing positions were rather neatly staked out. On what must have been a rather slack day in the Court of Common Pleas in 1345 counsel raised the question of how courts should discharge their function under the rule of law, arguing that if they did not do as they had in the past nobody would know what the law was. This provoked a judge called Hilary, an early legal iconoclast, to tell him what the law was: 'It is the will of the justices.' Stonore, another judge, was obviously rather shocked by this, and emphatically contradicted him: 'Not at all; law is reason.' The discussion proceeded, raising the question of the relationship between reason and precedent, the majority view being that precedents had to give way to reason. More or less the same discussion has been going on ever since, though very few judges or professional lawyers have joined the ranks of the iconoclasts. Perhaps the most celebrated iconoclast was Jeremy Bentham, who claimed that the common law was simply a myth. Judges made law as one controls a dog, waiting until the animal does something wrong and then beating it; he was doing battle with the ghost of Sir William Blackstone, the eighteenth-century jurist, who took Stonore's line.

In more modern times legal iconoclasm came to be developed in American legal thought in what is known as the American realist movement, which was a product of the 1920s and 1930s, and the spirit of Hilary was revived by Judge Jerome Frank, who enthusiastically joined the movement. American legal education had come to be dominated by a very strong version of the theory of legal science, and the realists rebelled against this. The ideal picture of a legal decision associated with legal science was that it involved the application of a determinate legal rule to some facts to produce a decision; we may present this in the form $R \times F = D$. With varying degrees of emphasis the realists argued that this was an *unreal* picture of how adjudication worked. Sometimes the emphasis was placed upon the uncertainties which in real life surround 'F' in the equation, the 'facts', and this version of realism has been called 'fact scepticism'. So, it might be said, in real life it is always possible that 'the facts' to which the rule is applied do not correspond with reality, or have been manipulated by the judge in order to produce a certain result. Facts do not, as it were, sit about meekly waiting to have rules applied to them; facts are things which lawyers and courts construct, not things they find. This is implied by 'fact scepticism', and, in various forms, is a common philosophical position. More typically, American realism involved various forms of what has been christened 'rule scepticism'. These involved minimizing the degree to which legal rules and doctrines are capable of conditioning the result of a case, or do in fact do so. The uncertainties surrounding what the rules and doctrines are, and the fact that legal reasoning, whether based upon authority or upon common-sense rationality, relies upon inconclusive reasons, produces a situation in real life in which the court often, or perhaps always, has a choice as to which way to go. Realists thus attacked what they called the myth of legal certainty, and Judge Jerome Frank, who was in the hands of analysts at the time, even attributed the search for legal certainty to an infantile pursuit of a father figure. Rule scepticism could be and was developed in a radical form in which, so the argument went, the official legal reasons for decisions should be viewed as a sort of window-dressing.

So the picture of legal decision taking offered by radical realism is that it is always some factor other than the legal rule that conditions the decision. This other factor ('OF'), according to a slightly frivolous version of the theory, might be the state of the judge's digestion. So the picture becomes OF (never R) $\times$ F = D. A fact sceptic would replace 'F' by something else, perhaps 'FCC' ('facts as constructed by the court'.) Another way of putting all this would be to say that the explanation for legal decisions must always be sought in factors other than those offered formally in their support; there is, we might say, always a story behind the headlines.

Legal realism developed for two basic reasons. The first is that the sheer scale of the American legal system, with its hundreds upon hundreds of courts and judges, and its massive production of reported cases, produced a situation in which the cohesion of the system began to break down. A relatively small common law system, such as that of England and Wales, can maintain a relatively cohesive professional tradition in which the notion that there is a right answer to most or even all legal problems does not so obviously jar with experience. For in such conditions there may in fact be a high degree of agreement and consensus as to which legal answers are right and which are wrong. In America this was not the position; thus, for example, in the vast mass of reported cases you could very often find decisions favouring either point of view in a legal controversy. The realist movement may be seen in part as a reaction to this. The second is that the theory of legal science, which realism attacked, was associated with the idea that it was possible by the use of reason to discover objectively valid principles of right and wrong to be applied to social behaviour, and the theory really viewed law as a branch of ethics. Indeed legal science was a version of the theory of objective natural law. By the time that American legal realism was developing general belief in objective ethical standards had waned, and so had the notion that the law was properly viewed as a branch of ethics, and the rise of realism reflects this.

In its extreme dogmatic form realism, like all forms of radical scepticism, appears to be incapable of proof or disproof, though numerous modern writers in the critical tradition naïvely assert that its truth has actually been demonstrated. But the same may be said for dogmatic legal science; and today there is a sense in which everyone, or almost everyone, has become an American realist in that they would concede that R × F = D is indeed an idealized or oversimplified picture of the nature of a judicial decision, that an element of choice enters into many or even perhaps all decisions, and that the factors which affect the outcome of cases may include some which have no official status. A practical result of the influence of realist scepticism is that scholars engage in research which is 'realist' in that it seeks to discover what really happens, not simply what, officially, ought to happen. For example, in criminal trials the law says that it is improper to engage in bargaining in which the accused trades a plea of guilty in return for undertakings as to the length of his sentence, or the dropping of more serious charges. So an accused might plead guilty to manslaughter if assured of a sentence of no more than five years if a murder charge is dropped. Such a system, virtually normal in America, is open to much abuse, and the official view is that 'plea-bargaining' does not (with some minor exceptions) go on here. But research in the realist tradition will not be put off by this, but investigate the reality of the matter, which may be that, in disguise, it does. Again in the same tradition one might investigate whether the political affiliations of judges influence their decisions, although the official theory is that they ought not to do so. At a moderate level realism only in effect amounts to a recognition that the rule of law is an ideal, not a picture of reality.

In more recent times legal iconoclasm has taken a new turn by becoming associated with Marxist theories of law, which appear to have had no influence at all on the pre-war realists. Whilst realism to various degrees casts doubt upon the attainability of the rule of law, Marxists go further in viewing belief in the idea as being a device, whose function it is to make the legal system, which is in reality a mechanism of oppression, appear morally legitimate to its victims. So whereas an extreme rule sceptic views the rule of law as a rather silly myth, the Marxist goes further and sees it as a highly important myth. It serves to increase the deference and respect paid to judicial decisions, and thereby bolsters up the legal system in its work of oppression. In modern times there has developed, most notably again in

American law schools, a form of iconoclastic legal theory essentially based upon combining the established realist tradition with notions derived from social theorists in the Marxist tradition and ideas derived from modern literary criticism. It has come to be known as the critical legal studies movement. This has generated a level of controversy in some law schools which may strike outsiders as strange, but it must be appreciated that in America the law is viewed by some of its exponents as a sort of secular religion forming the very basis of American society, and so those who engage in radical criticism of law are viewed as heretics were viewed in former times, fit only for the stake. Unlike the earlier realists, many who belong to the movement conceive of it as a political movement in that it is thought to be capable of affecting the distribution of power; this is consistent with the view they take of devotees of the rule of law. To date there is not the least sign of the movement having any effects outside academia, but these are early days. Controversy has been encouraged by the effective use of parody and ridicule by some authors in the tradition, and by the arrogance of language of others.

It is not possible to provide an official list of the tenets of the critical legal studies movement. Some of its members have merely continued the more radical realist tradition, seeking to show that legal rules and doctrines do not condition or adequately justify legal decisions. This may be expressed by what is known in the trade as 'trashing'; you take a reported case and seek to demonstrate that the legal justifications offered for it are incoherent, contradictory, silly, or in some other way trash. But the object of trashing is not simply intellectual, but political; the aim is to deprive legal decisions, and through them the legal system as it stands, of moral legitimacy, and this aim is pursued because the system is viewed as one which perpetuates forms of social organization and distribution of power which are themselves evil. Other writers have developed the idea, again derived from Marxist social theory, that legal doctrines generally both reflect views as to the nature of the world we live in and the society we inhabit, and serve to confirm and perpetuate existing social arrangements, which are, to those of radical persuasion, oppressive. To give a simplified example, the traditional doctrine of the law of contract presupposes that individuals have freedom of choice, and that in the absence of obvious forms of bullying and trickery the contracts they make are the ones they freely choose to make; hence they can hardly grumble if it turns out that they do not like the result. So, according to this way of thinking, this ideology embodied in contract doctrine, a stoker in the awful conditions obtaining in the engine room of a Victorian steamship in the Red Sea was there because he freely chose to be there. The conception of law as ideology, as in a sense conditioning how we think, and indeed behave, can be developed in a variety of different ways in conjunction with the notion that existing social arrangements, in particular those associated with capitalism, are fundamentally defective. To date the most interesting work in this genre has been historical, and principally directed towards attempts to understand the way criminal law, viewed as an ideology, functioned in earlier centuries.

The critical legal studies movement also embodies a visionary element. This starts from a rejection of the idea that existing legal structures and the social arrangements which go with them are in some sense defensible as morally right, or just, or appropriate to the state of the world we live in; instead they serve to bolster up and create a world we could well do without. So if through education there can be an escape from their dominance the whole structure will crumble and lose its power to control us. Indeed some writers have even claimed that this has begun to happen. What is to follow is however not made at all clear, but that is a general feature of utopianism.

LAW AND OTHER DISCIPLINES: LEGAL HISTORY

The critical legal studies movement involves then both an attitude to law as it exists as essentially evil and the application of social theory principally derived from writers in the Marxist tradition to the study of law. The academic study of law may obviously involve a variety of other disciplines, whose contribution to the subject may be inserted into traditional courses such as contract law, or property law, or be made the subject of special courses of their own.

We have seen that law is in its nature a product of the past, and one school of thought argues that it is really quite impossible to come to any level of legal understanding without studying the history of law. So courses in legal history commonly feature in legal education. Legal history may be purely doctrinal, seeking to trace the chronology of the development of particular legal doctrines and the way in which they came to be, at various times, part of the intellectual stock of ideas of professional lawyers. Or it may concentrate on the evolution of legal procedures and legal institutions, such as the courts or the legal profession, or attempt to relate procedural and institutional changes to doctrinal change. History is of course engaged not simply in telling tales, but also in explanation, and legal historians then face problems of a theoretical kind which are similar to those involved in the study of contemporary law. Can legal decisions be explained only in doctrinal terms? Or should the historian, like the legal realist, search outside the law for the story behind the headlines, attempting to relate legal change to the general historical context. Is trashing a great case of the past an intellectually rewarding exercise? Much work in legal history has concentrated on medieval law, and at this period most of the relevant source material is legal in character; for the fifteenth century, for example, we have literally tons by weight of legal records, but not a single personal diary, and only a handful of private letters. So the history of medieval society has been built up to a considerable extent out of legal materials, presumably distorting our view of that society. But for more modern periods a mass of non-legal evidence exists which can be used to throw light on legal developments, and its employment may elucidate theoretical disputes about the character of modern law. Historical studies of the history of criminal law, in particular, have also turned into a test bed for Marxist legal theory.

What might be called traditional legal history concentrates upon branches of the common law developed by the courts, for example contract law or property law. A wider conception of legal history is not of course so limited. As well as being concerned with legal arrangements outside the common law system, for example those operating in a variety of local courts, such as the stannary courts of the West Country miners, it will also be concerned with the history of legal arrangements introduced by legislation, for example by the factory legislation of the Victorian period. Broadening the scope of legal history opens up a whole range of fascinating subjects, many of them to date virtually unexamined. One example must suffice. At the beginning of the nineteenth century there existed virtually no law dealing with safety at sea. The nineteenth century did see the development of a body of law embodied in what were called Passenger Acts dealing with safety on emigrant ships, which has been fairly thoroughly investigated, and made the basis for a distinguished book on the rise of government in this period. There was also evolved a body of more general safety law designed to protect sailors as well as passengers. Why was this law evolved? What effects did it have on maritime safety? We must remember it all culminated in the loss of the *Titanic*, so perhaps it made very little difference at all. How did it relate to traditional common law and criminal law? How can this body of law be related, if at all, to the massive economic developments of this period? Did the law really help the sailors, or, as sceptics might think, merely serve to keep them quiet?

LAW AND PHILOSOPHY

We have already met the philosophical study of law, which turns up in law course under such names as 'Jurisprudence', 'Legal Philosophy' and 'Legal Theory'. The subject matter of such courses falls into two distinct categories. The first concerns general philosophical enquiries into the nature of the phenomenon of law itself; the traditional way of describing these enquiries is to say that they are attempts to answer the general question 'What is law?' This is something of an indigestible mouthful of a question, which needs cutting up before chewing, and if we do this we find that general jurisprudence is largely concerned with attempts to analyse and make more intelligible our notions of justice, of legal obligation, and of the rule of law.

Enquiries into the notion of justice have long featured in political and moral philosophy, and have an obvious interest for lawyers, more particularly because the ideas involved are deeply embedded in legal thought and reasoning. Curiously enough, however, law courses of a philosophical nature currently do not concentrate attention upon justice. In a sense there exists no special legal form of either of these two disciplines. Legal study does however throw up its distinctive problems over the conception of justice and its relationship with law, one of which is commonly discussed in relation to the analysis of legal obligation – is an unjust law binding, and in any event what does this mean? Another distinctive problem concerns the claim that pursuit of the ideal of the rule of law will tend to produce just laws, there being some intrinsic connection between law and justice. Of course there are many other questions which can be asked.

So far as legal obligation or duty is concerned one obvious feature of law is that it purports to render certain conduct obligatory; if something 'is the law', you have to do it. Now law is not the only source of obligations in society. We have family obligations, such as the obligation to attend family weddings and funerals, and the obligation to take the children on holiday each year. We have ethical obligations, such as the obligation in general to tell the truth and keep our promises, and many people feel obliged in some way to make gifts to charitable causes. Then there are religious obligations, which require some people to attend mass, or confess their sins to the priest, and obligations arising out of gratitude and friendship. And although we might not use the word obligation to describe them, there are powerful controls over our conduct arising out of fashion and etiquette. Many people find it extremely hard, if not impossible, to go to a party in boring clothes, and rules as to how one eats food, or lays a table are, by many people, quite rigidly observed. Then there are curious obligations in special groups, such as cricket clubs, or freemasons' lodges. So social life is shot through with obligations and duties of one kind and another, and investigations into the nature of legal obligation seek to identify what is special to legal obligations, what makes legal control, or legal obligation, different from other controls. Perhaps a successful enquiry here will tell us how precisely law in all societies differs from other forms of control, and enable us to put our finger upon what is distinctive about law as a mode of social ordering. One sort of answer relates legal obligation to organized coercion; others feel uneasy with a theory which selects so sordid a feature as the hallmark of law.

We have already had occasion to mention some of the difficulties which surround the notion of the rule of law, and the major thrust of general philosophical studies of law at the present time has taken the form of discussions of this conception, concentrating attention in particular upon the nature of judicial decisions. The controversies which surround the concept of the rule of law are closely asssociated too with controversies over the ideals of political liberalism, with which the theory of the rule of law came to be associated in the eighteenth and nineteenth centuries. In Britain liberalism is under constant attack from those of the left, whilst in America, where for all practical purposes the left does not exist except in intellectual circles, it is also under constant attack from the right. The political signific-ance attached to philosophical enquiries into the rule of law keeps the subject vigorously alive, and in the USA much controversy surrounds the activities of the Supreme Court which has very considerable political power under the constitution. If the court is to be viewed as a judicial organ, and not simply as a non-elected and consequently undemocratic legislature, some theory has to be found which reconciles its activities with the rule of law.

In addition to philosophical problems about law of a general nature, many more particular philosophical problems arise in legal study. For example, in tort law, the law of compensation for civil injuries (excluding breaches of contracts and trusts), the courts have made much use of the notion of *causation*. Indeed one approach which is found in the case law makes the idea central: people who *cause* loss to others should compensate them even if it is not clear that there has been any intention to injure, or any negligence. But what on earth does cause mean? We use the idea every day of the week, but our ability to use the idea is not matched by ability to analyse the notion in any very satisfactory way. There is therefore a large philosophical literature on the subject, and some have argued that the notion of causation is quite unintelligible; this is matched by a massive case law in which courts have attempted to make sense of the idea and use it in the law. Similar problems arise in criminal law. Suppose A stabs B, and B dies but would not have died if the doctor treating his case had not been so drunk at the time that the treatment he gave made his patient very much worse. Has A caused B's death? Another example of a particular problem involves the notion of intention. In many parts of the criminal law individuals are liable for results which they *intend*, and again we use this idea commonly in everyday life. But its analysis is not at all easy, and raises philosophical problems, centring upon the ways in which we think about human actions, which have never been satisfactorily resolved. Philosophical problems are like that; there are questions but never any perfect answers.

LAW AND THE SOCIAL SCIENCES

Sociology attempts both to develop general theories as to the nature of social organization and to engage in empirical studies designed, in the light of some theoretical hypothesis, to discover what actually happens in our society. Both activities tend to be in a sense subversive, for what emerges is often at odds with generally received views, and with what passes as the common sense of the matter. Some people find this upsetting, and others may be irritated by the fact that some sociologists adopt a rather hectoring tone in revealing in an olympian way The Truth about the world we live in. The subject has also suffered from the fact that its jargon (and all academic subjects have their own jargon) tends to be used by the undistinguished merely to mystify and confuse. What are called socio-legal studies have however come to play a considerable role in the academic study of the law, and are likely to continue to do so. To date interest in sociological high theory has tended to become associated with the critical legal studies movement. So far as empirical work is concerned there is a long tradition of enquiry into criminology and penology. At its most basic the former investigates the causes of crime and tries to come up with explanatory or predictive theories, whereas penology is concerned to investigate the effects of penal measures on human conduct. In these two areas many now feel that some of the questions being asked in the past were themselves somewhat silly ones, and that this may explain the lack of dramatic success. In more recent times empirical investigations into how the law works today, and has worked in the past, have produced some distinguished work outside these two traditional fields, and obviously work of a sociological character which deals with legal institutions and practices is immediately relevant to lawyers and to their legal education, although time is too short to turn law students into competent sociologists. Some universities and polytechnics make a particular effort to incorporate socio-legal studies into the curriculum.

Economics is the other social science which has in modern times had an important impact upon academic legal study, and one that is likely to increase in the future. The law and economics movement, though it can be traced back historically to pioneers such as the utilitarian philosopher Jeremy Bentham (1748–1832) and the political economist Adam Smith (1723–90) originated in its modern form in law schools in the USA. It has only very recently begun to have any influence upon legal education here. The idea that legal rules and institutions can have economic effects in society is hardly open to question. For example, the law requiring the use of seat belts in cars is generally thought to have had an immediate effect in reducing admissions to casualty wards in NHS hospitals, thereby reducing costs; arguably by keeping more young people alive it might in the long term add to NHS costs as those saved become elderly and return for geriatric care. Of course any attempt to work out the cost-benefit analysis would need to take into account other gains and losses. For example, the saved driver would return to work, pay taxes and thus contribute to the NHS in the intervening period. Plainly the law can be studied in this way, and the law economics movement has attempted to use both the empirical and theoretical methods developed by economics to increase understanding of the law, and of its social significance. For example, the criminal law can be viewed through the eyes of an economist as essentially a pricing mechanism, and knowledge developed elsewhere by economists on the working of pricing mechanisms may help us to understand both how the law currently operates and how it might operate more effectively. Again empirical studies of the working of the system of accident compensation may suggest that it fails to achieve the objects attributed to the system in the most efficient way, and if this is so then we might be better off with some other system. It is hard to see any reason why economic analysis along these lines should not be regarded as valuable, though of course the results of a particular enquiry may be controversial.

The law and economics movement, as developed in the USA, has become engaged however in more general controversy, and this for a variety of reasons, the principal one being, I suspect, the unattractive nature of the creature who sits at the centre of the web of economic ideas involved: economic man, whose ruthless pursuit, within the terms of his own subjective rationality, of personal self-interest is supposed somehow to make the world a better place. Much economic theory centres upon the word *somehow*. Another objection has been that some of the devotees of the movement have tended to view the pursuit of economic efficiency as a goal or end in itself and one which ought to prevail over other values, a notion which some find morally un-acceptable. Yet another is that the movement has tended to be very strongly committed to the view that the free market is the best mechanism for the distributiuon of resources, and this naturally gives rise to controversy with those who argue that important values are best served by a greater degree of state interference in the operations of the market. Some writers belonging to the movement have applied their theories interestingly, though controversially, to legal history, claiming, for example, that the history of the common law can be viewed as a process in which economically efficient solutions have tended to triumph over inefficient ones by a sort of natural selection. In one form or another it is probable that the movement will have a considerable impact upon historical studies in the future.

COMPARATIVE LAW

One way of trying to understand a social institution and to study it critically is to try to step outside it. Historical studies have often been presented in this light as a way of understanding not the past but the present. Comparative law involves this approach, and is a long-established subject in law schools. Some years back now the study of ancient Roman law was a normal part of the law curriculum, and one form its study took was comparative; for example, the Oxford syllabus used to include a paper on the comparison between the Roman law of delict and the English law of torts, with some slight study of French law thrown in. Today the study of ancient Roman law has much declined, and a comparative law course is more likely to concentrate upon aspects of modern continental legal systems, which belong to the civil law tradition, and such courses essentially involve comparison between legal *traditions*. They may have a purely practical value: with greater involvement in Europe and the law of the European Community lawyers will need, more and more, to be able at least to communicate with civil lawyers. At an intellectual level seeing how other societies manage their legal arrangements may both open ones eye's to defects in our own system, and point to ways of reform and improvement. If this latter function is to be served comparison must be with a legal tradition in operation in a society reasonably similar to our own, and for this and other reasons courses in comparative law usually touch rather lightly upon legal traditions of a very different nature, such as Islamic or Hindu law.

Comparative legal studies conducted in undergraduate courses obviously face difficulties over languages. It is very difficult to acquire any great understanding of legal materials unless they can be read in the original. They also face difficulties over superficiality; given shortage of time this is inevitable. The same problem in fact arises in the case of all attempts to widen the scope of legal education; thus a course in legal history has to be very selective indeed in the topics and periods it covers, and a course in law and economics has to grapple with the fact that most students will come to it largely ignorant of elementary economic theory. But difficulties of this kind do not seriously undermine the value of the attempt to widen the scope of legal study, though they may produce problems of organization, for the aim is that of introducing students to new ways of thinking about the law which they can explore further if they wish, and of breaking down insular and uncritical attitudes to the profession of the law. No doubt much of the seed will fall on stony ground, but that is unhappily true of much that is rightly done in education.

8

The Future of the Law

Futurology is a notoriously unreliable activity, but nevertheless we may take a risk and conclude this invitation to law with some brief consideration of its future. For there is a school of thought, though hardly yet a strong one, which has suggested that law as we know it is dying, a view which is pessimistic or optimistic according to how one views the matter. The same idea in a less startling form can be expressed by saying that the nature of law is changing in a radical way. Such a view of the future is inevitably related to a view of the past, and to the idea that by studying it broadly we can discover definite patterns of change

THEORIES OF LEGAL EVOLUTION

There is indeed a long tradition of attempts to work out general theories of legal development, which enable us to place ourselves at the appropriate point on a sort of chart of legal evolution. We have already met one such theory, that of Sir Henry Maine, set out in his *Ancient Law*. He argued that societies which had progressed (and most had not) had seen a movement from status to contract, and he placed the Victorian society to which he belonged in the era of contract. Maine was careful to say that this had *hitherto* been the case, leaving open the possibility that in the future life might change and the predominance of contract law perhaps go; Maine was no futurologist. He also developed an evolutionary theory as to how the law was changed, and did not everywhere resemble that of the Medes and Persians. He detected a sequence in the mechanisms of change. First used were fictions or myths, second equity, and then legislation; again Victorian society lay in the era of legislation. It is not surprising that theories of legal evolution were popular in this period, which also produced Charles Darwin's *Origin of the Species*, though Maine himself does not seem to have been influenced by Darwin. Another Victorian scholar who toyed with ideas of this character was A. V. Dicey in his still highly readable book *Law and Public Opinion in Nineteenth Century Britain*. Dicey was particularly interested in Maine's third mechanism of legal change, legislation, and attempted to explain the changes in the way legislation was used in the nineteenth century by reference to movements in public opinion. He thought that in Britain, though not in all societies, it was public opinion which in this period conditioned legal change. Scholars interested in the early history of law and in legal anthropology have also made much play with the idea of stages in legal evolution and attempts to relate them to stages of social and economic development, and there is a considerable literature on what used, somewhat rudely, to be called primitive law.

Outside the common law world the most influential writing in this general area comes from the German social theorist Max Weber (1864–1920). Weber was not particularly interested in working out historical sequences in the evolution of law. Instead he tried to analyse the nature of legal phenomena by relating them to 'ideal types' to which actual phenomena might, as it were, approximate. His ideas were very complex, but the flavour may be given by this brief account. Consider legal decisions. These might be taken irrationally, as when guilt or innocence is settled by the use of some supernatural device outside the scope of human thought, such as the ordeal of fire or water, used in the common law up to 1215; this to Weber is legal irrationality, and he distinguished it as formal. Or decisions might be taken by reference to the gut reaction of the judge to the facts of the particular case without any attempt to refer the decision to general rules or principles; this is what we call palm tree justice, the decision being taken in this way by the judge sitting under the palm tree. This too Weber called legal irrationality, but he distinguished it as substantive irrationality. To Weber the irrationality depended upon the failure to refer the decision to general rules of any kind. Alternatively decisions might be taken rationally, that is by reference to general rules and principles. But there were different types of rationality. The rules might not be identifiably legal, for example decisions might be taken by reference to moral notions, or ideas of justice; this was however rationality, and he distinguished it as substantive. Or decisions might be taken by reference to a body of abstract concepts and rules which were the product of the thought of a special group, the lawyers. This he called formal logical rationality, which we have already met under another name as legal science. Now if you apply this scheme of ideas to everyday decisions in the courts, what might be called the official line (embodied in the notion of the rule of law) is that they are in the business of formal logical legal rationality, but the reality of the matter is that such decisions only imperfectly coincide with this ideal type; elements of the other ideal types also are to be found in legal decisions. But at certain periods one type may predominate, and to this extent Weber's ideas can be used in a theory of legal evolution.

In modern times theories of legal evolution, which involve the idea that in some sense the future is determined, have largely been influenced by Marxism, and surface in the world of legal studies in the critical legal studies movement. A writer who is something of a prophet of the movement and who has developed ideas of this character, using conceptions in part derived from Weber, is R. M. Unger; he has also toyed with futurology and utopianism. Of course a certain vagueness necessarily hangs over both, and in any event it is peculiarly hard for contemporaries to detect movements in history which are taking place in their own times. No parties were held at the time to celebrate the end of the Dark Ages, or bells rung at the close of the medieval period. But without my attempting either to reproduce or criticise the more elaborate theories, a little reflection will I think suggest that in

England at least there are signs of fairly radical changes in the place of law in our scheme of social and political organization.

VICTORIAN LEGAL IDEOLOGY

We can approach this possibility by looking first at legal education. As we have seen doctrinal legal education, which forms the central core of legal education, reflects the theory of legal science, and the period during which this theory flourished in the history of the common law was the second half of the nineteeenth century, a period which is often referred to as the classical period of the common law. Precisely why is a difficult question, but there is no doubt but that very much of the intellectual stock of ideas of common lawyers today comes from this period, and the traditions of legal education which have come to be established tend to emphasise the legacy of the nineteenth century. Thus most of the ideas a law student comes across in contract law, tort law and criminal law, and many in constitutional law, take the nineteenth century as the starting point; indeed many cases which are central in legal education come from this period. This is so too of the concept of the rule of law, which is expounded as a commentary upon A. V. DIcey's statement of the theory in his *Law of the Constitution*, first published in 1885. Furthermore this emphasis upon the nineteenth century is an emphasis upon the common law developed by judicial decision in the courts, and is not concerned with the history of the legislation of the period, the subject which fascinated A. V. Dicey, but has not much fascinated most of his successors in academic law. The scheme of ideas which dominate legal education are the same ideas as dominate the thinking of professional lawyers, and they have filtered through society generally. In short we tend to think about law in much the same way as did Dicey or his contemporaries. Our legal ideology is Victorian.

In fact the classical era of the common law was, paradoxically, an era during which it began to be relatively less important. The rise in the belief in both the practicability and desirability of state intervention to redress social wrongs and improve matters generally, together with the rise of expert professional central and local bureaucracies, was already transforming the world in which the common law operated. In this century the process has continued, and has been accelerated by the two wars, with their centrally managed economies and hugely inflated level of detailed regulation. This process has been accompanied by the multiplication of agencies which are in fact courts (such as rent tribunals) which operate outside the common law; almost as soon as the common law had triumphed over its old rival courts, new ones were invented. In this process power has passed to the civil service operating under the Cabinet, and over considerable periods the Cabinet has been in a position to control Parliament. The change in the scale and scope of government over the last century-and-a-half or so, together with changes in the working of the British Constitution, has obviously altered the place of traditional common law in the scheme of things. Yet it is not clear that it has altered the way lawyers think about the law. For example, judges, or at least red judges, remain the godlike creatures they were in 1860, but today it is the mandarins of the civil service who are the real Mr Bigs in the scheme of government. Many red judges spend most of their time dealing with boring and unimportant squabbles between motor insurance companies and trying burglars, both jobs which could in reality be handled by any intelligent twenty-five-year-old without anyone noticing the difference. Of course from time to time they get their teeth into something more exciting, as for example when they leave court and conduct judicial enquiries like Lord Scarman's enquiry into the Brixton riots, surely the most important thing he ever did as a judge, except that in a sense he did not do it as a judge.

Now it is not implausible to suppose that the changes mentioned, and no doubt others, have in some respects altered the character of law in our society generally. Law, it might be argued, has become principally an instrument of the bureaucracy. Now from the point of view of bureaucracy government through law has its attractions; it makes for efficiency of administration and a quiet life, for the respect accorded to courts may increase the degree to which the activities of government will be acquiesced in by the governed. But looked at from another viewpoint the restrictions imposed by adherence to the spirit of the rule of law can be viewed as simply a nuisance. This attitude was most obviously prevalent and openly admitted in wartime conditions. Hence during the Second World War government, operating through the forms of law, acquired discretionary and indeed arbitrary powers of a draconian nature, for example to imprison individuals without any form of trial whatsover for indefinite periods of time, powers which were used in thousands of cases. These powers were indeed conferred by law, being passed through Parliament, but they did not produce government under law in the sense required by the ideal of the rule of law.

This is not merely a phenomenon of wartime; the use of law in opposition to the ideal of the rule of law has today become commonplace. It takes various forms. One is the passing of laws which confer very wide discretionary powers upon officials, in effect making their activities within broadly defined limits outside legal control, or indeed public scrutiny of any kind. Another is the creation of criminal laws which are extremely widely drafted, so that in reality the decision as to what is to be treated as criminal, and what not, rests with the discretion of the prosecuting authority or government. Another is the establishment of mechanisms which move decisions from open court to meetings behind closed doors. The system of release of prisoners on parole is one example here: the length of a prisoner's sentence is no longer determined in court but in committee. Another example is the increase in judicial hearings *in camera*. A few years back an individual, the double agent or triple agent or quadruple agent Blake, for how can we ever tell, was, in peacetime, sentenced in secret to forty-two years in prison. No public protest took place about this almost incredible occurrence at all. To this day, although Blake long since decamped to Russia, the details have not been revealed. Another technique is so to organize matters that access to the law is in fact not available, or only available on terms which in practice rule it out for most people most of the time, or when they need it. Thus people arrested for very serious crimes, who really need lawyers, are not allowed to have them promptly if officials say no. Denial of access has, for example, dramatically reduced the effectiveness of the remedy of habeas corpus. Again civil litigation generally is largely unused in England because of the costs and hazards involved.

If you keep your eye on the papers you will endlessly see examples of this general process. A happy hunting ground for illustrations is the operation of the Official Secrets Act. Obviously government under law will only flourish in a vigilant society, and the whole function of the protection of official secrets, introduced originally in the name of security against foreign enemies, is to prevent the public being vigilant. Government after government promises to amend the law; nobody actually does so, and if and when the Act is repealed and replaced it is virtually certain that the job will be done in such a way as to increase control over information of importance whilst relaxing control in areas which do not much matter.

Where then does law fit into this rather gloomy picture? It is not in the least likely that in the foreseeable future the scope of governmental intervention in our lives will diminish, though the forms through which it is exercised may well change. Nor is it in the least likely that the tradition of governing through legal forms will diminish in importance. What is, however, possible is that government through law will come to be more acutely in opposition to the ideal of the rule of law than is the case at present, and if this happens law, in the sense required by the ideal of the rule of law, will die. What will be left will be the rule of a type of law against which citizens will need protection, not a type of law which provides them with protection. There is nothing visionary in such an idea; in the Second World War law, as a protector of personal liberty, did die; for those detained the courts did nothing whatsoever. A perception of this general problem has been the development in the courts of administrative law, which is the branch of law which purports to contain the activities of officialdom within the bounds of law. Another expression of this perception has been the enthusiasm, in some circles, for some form of legally entrenched bill of rights. The survival of government through law in the sense required by the ideal of the rule of law will depend to a very considerable extent upon the enthusiasm with which the legal profession addresses itself to the job of reinterpreting the ideal into a form which is realistic and effective in the world of today, and to achieve this will require a determined effort to escape from the somewhat empty rhetoric which is a legacy of the fossilized Victorian ideology of the profession. There are some hopeful signs, and the job is surely not an impossible one.

9

Where Next?

Where do we go next? There are three useful courses of action. The first is to do some more reading, the second is to try to have some contact with the practice of the law, and the third is to discover some information about how you become a lawyer.

SUGGESTIONS FOR FURTHER READING

For someone considering the academic study of the law what is needed is reading which shows that the study of law can be intellectually interesting and which gives an impression of how law can be studied and thought about. It is not a good idea to begin with a straight law book; they tend to be repulsive unless read in conjunction with the study of the cases upon which they are based, and this requires both guidance and access to a set of law reports. Indeed few people actually do read law books in the sense in which you read a novel or a biography. They use them as a sort of map to less organized materials. What follows in the way of suggestions may not suit everyone, and my advice would be to drop any book on this list which strikes you as boring. However, if you find all these books boring I suspect law is not for you. Many of the books recommended are available in paperback, and all should be easy to get hold of through a public library.

On what sort of book should you start? One possibility is to start with books about trials, a form of literature with which most people will have some familiarity. Many accounts of trials treat the trial as a piece of drama without delving very much into the way in which the law and life are intertwined; the main focus of such books is to question the validity of the conviction or acquital. Others, however, raise more general issues about the law. One trial which is particularly well covered by books of the second type is that of Dr John Bodkin Adams. Sybille Bedford's classic *The Best We Can Do* (London, 1958), which deals with this case, has now been joined by a book by the trial judge, Lord Patrick Devlin, *Easing the Passing* (London, 1985), which is really an essay in the ideal of the trial under the rule of law. If you like this you might also like his book *The Judge* (Oxford, 1979). Another study of a criminal case which attempts to raise some wider issues about the working of the law is my own *Cannibalism and the Common Law* (Chicago, 1984; London, 1986), which deals with the famous case in 1884 in which two sailors killed and ate a ship's boy after a shipwreck, and ended up on trial for murder. There are many other cases covered in the Notable British Trials series, and the ones to choose are those that raise questions of law as well as questions of fact, or which touch on wider issues. Examples are the volumes dealing with Ronald True (ed. D. Carswell, London, 1925), with William Joyce, (ed. J. W. Hall, London, 1946) or with Bywaters and Thompson (ed. F. Young, London, 1923). If you like Victorian *causes célèbres* D. Woodruff's *The Tichborne Claimant* (London, 1957) is another example of this genre which is more than of passing interest. C. H. Rolph's edition of *The Trial of Lady Chatterley (R. v. Penguin Books Ltd* (London, 1961), which deals with the failure of a prosecution under the Obscene Publications Act of 1959 of Penguins for publishing D. H. Lawrence's novel, is again a book which deals with a trial of considerable historical importance, and is an excellent read.

Either as an alternative starting point, or after digging into some trial literature, you can try one of the relatively few books about the law which have achieved classic status; two which are still highly readable date from the Victorian period. They are

H. S. Maine's *Ancient Law* (London, 1861) and O. W. Holmes's *The Common Law* (Boston, 1881). Both authors were men of affairs: Maine served on the Viceroy's Council in British India, whilst Holmes became a celebrated Justice of the Supreme Court of the USA Much of what is said in both books is now thought to be mistaken, but both are still worth reading, amongst other reasons because they show how law can be thought about in a general and intellectually interesting way. If you like them then you could read more about Maine in G. Feaver's *From Status to Contract* (London, 1969), and about Holmes in M. de Wolfe Howe's *Justice Oliver Wendell Holmes* (Cambridge, Mass. 1951, 1963), which is interesting but too long. Another nineteenth-century classic is A. V. Dicey's *Law and Public Opinion in Nineteenth Century Britain* (London, 1905), and the same author's *Law of the Constitution* (9th edn, London, 1939) is by no means as daunting as it sounds. Books written more recently which have achieved both classic status and are readable are not easy to come by. A good case could, however, be made for H. L. A. Hart's *The Concept of Law* (Oxford, 1961), but this will only appeal if you have rather philosophical interests. It is, as such books go, very readable indeed.

Moving away from classics there are a number of guides to legal study, of which the best established is G. Williams's *Learning the Law* (11th edn, London, 1982); I should defer using such a book until you are beginning a law course, for they are designed solely as study guides and sources of useful information. There are also numerous general accounts of the English legal system, but these are mainly concerned to purvey useful information; a good comprehensive one is R. J. Walker's *The English Legal System* (6th edn, London, 1985), a beetle crusher if ever there was one. I should leave such books aside for the moment. A better start would be C. K. Allen's *Law in the Making* (7th edn, Oxford, 1964), but if you try this skip the theoretical introduction which is very heavy going. This is now a little out of date but still an excellent account of the way the law has evolved. Another book which covers some of the same ground and is something of a classic is E. H. Levi's *An Introduction to Legal*

Reasoning (Chicago, 1949), which has the additional merit of being of modest length.

There are now many books which are perfectly intelligible to a beginner which discuss particular branches of the law or aspects of law. One of the best is P. S. Atiyah's *Accidents, Compensation and the Law* (2nd edn, London, 1975). This belongs to the Law in Context series. Other volumes in this series which you might like are J. Eekelaar's *Family Law and Social Policy* (2nd edn, London, 1984), K. O'Donovan's *Sexual Divisions and the Law* (London, 1985) and G. Robertson's *Obscenity* (London, 1985). If this latter subject interests you you might also find *The Report of the Departmental Committee on Pornography and Film Censorship*, republished by the Cambridge University Press as B. Williams (ed.), *Obscenity and Film Censorship* (1981) interesting. There are a number of short books originating as the Hamlyn Lectures, and published by Stevens, which discuss particular aspects of the law and which are aimed at laymen. Good examples are B. Wootton's *Crime and the Criminal Law* (London, 1963), A. R. N. Cross's *Punishment, Prison and the Public* (London, 1971), and R. Dahrendorf's *Law and Order* (London, 1985). Lord Denning's numerous books are, like his judicial opinions, highly readable if somewhat eccentric; the best is perhaps his *The Discipline of the Law* (London, 1979), or some would say *The Family Story* (London, 1981). A. Paterson's *The Law Lords* (London, 1982) is a good introduction to socio-legal studies at a not too disagreeably theoretical level.

For those interested in the origin of law E. E. Evans-Prichard's anthropological classic *The Nuer* (Oxford, 1940) describes a successful society which lacks law, and S. Robert's *Order and Dispute* (London, 1979) provides a more general discussion. The best basic introduction to English legal history is J. H. Baker's *An Introduction to English Legal History* (2nd edn, London, 1979), though I am not sure that it is appropriate for a beginner. Philosophical interests can be pursued in H. L. A. Hart's *Punishment and Responsibility* (Oxford, 1968) and *Law, Liberty and Morality* (London, 1963). If you find either appealing you should also look into Lord Devlin's arguments presented in his *The*

Enforcement of Morality (London, 1965). R. Dworkin's views can be followed in his *Law's Empire* (London, 1986). A huge literature surrounds the criminal law and the related subjects of penology and criminology; two books which can be recommended are L. Radzinowicz and J. King's *The Growth of Crime* (London, 1979) and N. Walker's *Sentencing in a Rational Society* (London, 1972). A glance down the shelves of a public library will produce many others.

On the place of ideals generally in legal thought there is P. Stein and J. Shand's *Legal Values in Western Society* (Edinburgh, 1974). The best modern statement of the ideal of the rule of law (called legality) is in L. L. Fuller, *The Morality of the Law* (New Haven, 1964). A more elaborate presentation is F. A. Hayek's *Law, Legislation and Liberty* (Chicago, 1973–9), which combines a statement of liberal political philosophy with an attack on socialism as incompatible with liberty. Much the best introductions to legal iconoclasm in the marxist tradition are E. P. Thompson's *Whigs and Hunters* (London, 1975) and D. Hay's (and others') *Albion's Fatal Tree* (London, 1975, 1977). Both deal with eighteenth-century law, and the former contains a very interesting discussion of the rule of law as its conclusion. If you want to dig further into Marxist theories of law, H. Collins's book on this subject, *Marxism and the Law* (Oxford, 1982), makes things as clear as they are ever going to be. J. A. G. Griffiths's *The Politics of the Judiciary* (London, 1977) is a readable criticism of the judges for being too establishment-minded. The flavour of American realism is best caught from Jerome Frank's *Law and the Modern Mind* (London, 1949), and if you read it you need to know that Frank, in spite of his odd views, was a very good judge. The only general book on American critical legal studies is R. M. Unger's *The Critical Legal Studies Movement* (London, 1986), which is unhappily written in a style which sacrifices intelligibility in an attempt to convey a sense of mystical truth. A better feel for this particular writer's ideas might be derived from his *Law in Modern Society* (London, 1976) which is an attempt to fit contemporary law into an original theoretical framework of social theory, and is attractive to those who like this sort of thing;

as a professional historian I confess I personally do not. If you do, try to get hold of Max Weber's *Law in Economy and Society* (Cambridge, Mass., 1954); there is an edition by Max Rheinstein in the 20th. Century Legal Philosophy series published by the Harvard University Press.

Law is not just about ideas; it is also about people, and one important class of people involved are lawyers. Unhappily there are few good English legal biographies, but E. Majoribank's *Life of Sir Edward Marshall Hall* (London, 1929), H. Montgomery Hyde's *Norman Birkett* (London, 1964) and R. F. V. Heuston's *Lives of the Lord Chancellors 1885–1940* (London, 1964) are exceptions to the rule. There are hosts of poor ones, and numerous autobiographies, virtually none of any quality. There is a considerable lighter literature of the law, some of which gives a real flavour of the subject; the best example comprises A. P. Herbert's *Misleading Cases* (collected as *Uncommon Law* (London, 1935)), which both parody and illuminate legal reasoning.

Finally there are the newspapers and television, both of which endlessly pursue matters of legal interest, particularly issues which are topical. Anyone seriously interested in the law will find that not a day passes without new material being presented and discussed. For law reports the quality papers, especially *The Times*, and to a lesser extent the *Telegraph* and the *Independent*, are the best source; the *Guardian* goes in more for comment than reporting. Of course all papers tend to present their news packaged, and readers need to keep an eye out for this. The more squalid organs of the press are in their own way equally interesting in the attitudes they express to law and matters legal.

CONTACT WITH THE LEGAL PROFESSION

The courts are free and normally open to the public; visit them. All towns have a magistrates' court, and if you go along you can find out when it will be sitting. To go to a juvenile court you need to see the Clerk of the Court or write to him for permission. If you can organize a group you might be able to arrange a tour.

Larger towns have Crown courts, dealing with criminal business. Only the larger centres handle the more gory crimes like murder. If you live in London the Old Bailey is bursting with business, and you could also see the Court of Appeal, Criminal Division, in operation, which may amaze you. Civil cases go on in the county courts, which exist in many towns; you can check from the telephone book and ring to discover when they are sitting. The cases handled are the less financially important ones. Bigger cases go on in the High Court of Justice. This operates in numerous rooms in the Royal Courts of Justice in the Strand, and in a number of other larger towns, like Liverpool; again a little work on the phone book will reveal all. The civil Court of Appeal sits in London in the Royal Courts of Justice. The ultimate court of appeal is the House of Lords, but I should not trouble with it at this stage.

There are solicitors everywhere, organized in local law societies. If you do not know one enter any solicitor's office, explain your interest and ask for the name of the secretary of the local society. With a litle polite pushing you can usually persuade a solicitor to show you round and even let you work in the office for a few weeks to get an impression of what goes on. However, there are big differences in practices between rather sleepy country firms and the larger city firms. All attempts to see into the legal profession are made easier if you avoid hippy dress and look tidy and neat. You should also be able to contact solicitors at the local magistrates' court. Getting to know barristers is more difficult as there are not many of them, and most are based in London. Again you need to exploit any chances you get. Some circuit judges are helpful in talking to intending students; find out the name of a local one and try writing. You may also find that the Inns of Court (on which see below) will arrange tours of the Inn and opportunities to meet barristers.

There are other institutions which may interest you, prisons for example. Visiting prisons is a more complicated operation because of security and also because of a desire not to turn them into zoos. So a visit requires prior organization, normally of a group, and this is best set up by your school. Of course school societies can arrange talks by the local prison governor, or from such people as probation officers without these problems.

BECOMING A LAWYER

If you are considering becoming a lawyer then you should first of all obtain a copy of the Association of Graduate Careers Advisory Services booklet *The Legal Profession*. This can be obtained from Careers Offices and from the Central Services Unit, Crawford House Precinct Centre, Manchester M13 9EP (061-273-4233). The Manpower Services Commission also publish a booklet *Law* as no. 26 of their Choice of Careers publications; it is published by the Stationery Office (HMSO). This also publishes *Lawyers* which is a guide to legal careers in the civil service and *A Career in the Magistrates Courts*. If you want to find out about legal executives write to the Institute at Ilex House, Banhill Road, London SW2 4RW. *Barristers in Business* can be had from the Bar Association for Commerce at 63 Gt Cumberland Place, Bryanston Square, London W1H 7LJ. Armed with this literature you can begin to think about law as a career, and you will see that the easiest way to become a lawyer is to take a law degree course at a university or polytechnic, so you should find out about how you do this. It is also a good idea to look at *The Law Society's Gazette*, and *Counsel*, the two trade papers, and at *The New Law Journal*. You should be able to see these at a public library.

You should not rest content with your labours. Write to obtain copies of the current regulations governing the professions and whatever goodies are on offer. Those for solicitors can be obtained from The Law Society, 113 Chancery Lane, London WC2A 1PL, and the Law Society also publishes *A Guide for Articled Clerks* and *Training to be a Solicitor*. So write and ask for whatever is going; the letter may be addressed to the Secretary for Education and Training. Intending barristers – and I should strongly advise you not to make a choice between the branches of the profession without getting information about both – should write to the Council of Legal Education at 4 Gray's Inn

Place, London WC1R 5DX for the regulations and anything else they are giving away, and obtain *A Career at the Bar* either from the Council or from the Senate at 11 South Square, Gray's Inn, London WC1R 5EL. The Council publishes *Notes on How to Become a Barrister*. The regulations are published in the Calendar which is revised annually about June. If you are inclined towards the bar then you need to find out more about the financial assistance offered and about the Inns. You can if you wish write direct to the four Inns, addressing your letter to the Office of the Under Treasurer (in the case of the Inner Temple the Sub-Treasurer) and explaining that you are thinking of becoming a barrister. All four have Student Advisers. The addresses are Lincoln's Inn, London, WC2A 3TL, Inner Temple, EC4Y 7HL, Middle Temple, EC4Y 7HL, Gray's Inn, WC1R 5FU. The Senate also publishes a booklet on assistance over pupillage.

The required education for lawyers, whether intending to be barristers or solicitors, is divided into two stages. The first is called the Academic Stage, and the second the Vocational Stage. Let us take barristers first, and begin with the simplest route, which begins with taking a law degree at a university or polytechnic; if you do this and take the six 'core' subjects this completes the Academic Stage. Although there are some exceptions, you must however obtain a second class degree as a minimum. (If you take a recognized law degree or mixed degree but not all six subjects you can in some circumstances get exemptions in those you have done, and pick up the rest at the City University or Polytechnic of Central London; you need to check carefully about this.) The degree will of course take you three years at a minimum. You can join an Inn before completing this stage (there are some minimum requirements and you need to be of good character) and this is usually sensible during your first year at university or polytechnic, as you have to clock up terms by eating dinners in the Inn. The basic rule is that you have to keep eight terms before call to the bar and if you want to practise, four more after call. There are four terms each year and three dinners count as a term. So the sensible rule is join fairly early, say in your second year at university or polytechnic, and start eating. Early contact with the Inn is also useful in seeking out chambers in which they will accept you as a pupil. Indeed if you want to practise at the bar the more contact you have with the Inn the better.

Once over the hurdle of the Academic Stage then, if you want to practise as a barrister in this country, you take as the first part of the Vocational Stage a one-year course run by the Council of Legal Education at the Inns of Court School of Law. This includes practical exercises which you must complete satisfactorily. You then take the Bar Examination and if you pass you can then be called to the bar, and that makes you a barrister at law. But you still cannot practice as one without spending a year as an apprentice, this being called pupillage. The whole process therefore takes five years at a minimum; there are provisions for retakes and conditional passes in the bar examination. If you do not want to practise you do not have to attend the Inns of Court course or do pupillage; you just have to pass the bar examination.

You can however become a barrister without having a law degree, so long as you have a second class degree in something else, but you then have to satisfy the Academic Stage by taking a one-year diploma course in London in the core subjects, so that means six years in all at a minimum. You study for this either at the City University (Centre for Legal Studies, Northam Square, London EC1V 0HB) or the Polytechnic of Central London (Law School Registry, Red Lion Square, London WC1R 4SR). The bar is now virtually an all-graduate profession, but there are special arrangements for mature students without degrees, and arrangements for transfer to the bar by qualified solicitors. This last option is well worth considering; you qualify as a solicitor first and then transfer.

For an intending solicitor, taking a a law degree which includes the core subjects is the simplest route into the profession. But this does not completely satisfy the Academic Stage; it is still necessary to take Solicitors' Final Examination after having attended a one-year course either at the Law Society's own school of law or at one of a number of polytechnics. It is also necessary to serve a period of apprenticeship called articles, which is normally two years long, and this period is served normally after passing the Final. Eighteen months of this period must be after the Final is passed. What this means is that the time taken to qualify is around a year longer than for a barrister, par for the course being six years and not five, but you get a salary during articles which means that the lean years may be fewer. You can become a solicitor without taking a law degree, as is the case with the bar. Other graduates have to take the core subjects; if their degree includes none of them this will involve a one-year polytechnic course and thus extend the process of qualification to seven years. Those who have taken some of the core subjects in their degree may not have to attend a course but will still have to pass an examination in the subjects they have missed. It is also possible to become a solicitor without either taking a degree of any kind or waiting until you become a mature student. This hard route involves taking the Solicitors' First Examination, spending five years in articles and passing the Final, the time involved if all goes well being six years. There are also special arrangements for barristers, mature students and legal executives.

The regulations are complicated and can change, so there is no substitute for getting hold of them rather than relying on a short outline such as this. In particular if you are a mature student or have some notion that you may be a special case you should write and enquire. Tricky problems can arise for those who have blotted their copybook by acquiring a criminal record, and the professions understandably take a very dim view of any dishonest concealment, whilst, in my experience (I hasten to add second-hand) they are very reasonable about applicants who have outlived some isolated incident in the past. So come clean. Perhaps the most generally asked question is whether to proceed by the normal route, which involves taking a law degree which includes the core subjects, or to study some other subject at the degree stage. Taking the latter option will postpone final qualification for a year or perhaps a little more, and that is not a long time, though it obviously involves additional expense before earning begins. The main loss will be educational, but it has to be admitted that many very good lawyers have studied other subjects for degrees and, as it were, caught up later. Perhaps the critical question is how keen you are to take some other course than law at the degree level, bearing in mind that you will rarely have another chance. Taking degrees which include some but not all the core subjects is an option worth considering; it can cause virtually no loss of time, but the details need to be worked out in the light of the current regulations. As we have seen you can become a solicitor without a degree, but it really is the hard route. A second common question comes from women: what is the level of prejudice against them? Perhaps prejudice is the wrong word; institutionalised discrimination is what we are talking about. The solicitor's profession is a large one, and there is room for women applicants, given the level of application, so that it does not seem to present a very serious problem. The statistical position looks worse than it is felt to be by women solicitors. The figures for the bar are bad, and, perhaps more importantly, there is a sense of resistance. So women entering the legal profession need to ask about these matters and realize that they are still breaking into a male world. They should take with a big grain of salt protestations from the professions that everything in the garden is now lovely; it isn't. It does not of course follow that women cannot succeed as lawyers; they do. Finally anyone, male or female, thinking of the bar should seek as much advice as possible from younger barristers if they can possibly meet some. It is not a profession to join lightly, and you should not be overcome by the glamour. It is however for some very rewarding, and this not simply in financial terms.

Index

224

Index